U.S. Mergers and Acquisitions

Felix Lessambo

U.S. Mergers and Acquisitions

Legal and Financial Aspects

palgrave
macmillan

Felix Lessambo
Gabelli School of Business,
Accounting & Tax
Fordham University
New York, NY, USA

ISBN 978-3-030-85734-9 ISBN 978-3-030-85735-6 (eBook)
https://doi.org/10.1007/978-3-030-85735-6

This Palgrave Macmillan imprint is published by the registered company Springer Nature Switzerland AG
The registered company address is: Gewerbestrasse 11, 6330 Cham, Switzerland

Acknowledgments

Writing a book is always a challenge. But writing a book on US Mergers & Acquisitions, a more daring intellectual exercise.

I would like to thank my astoundingly supportive friends who motivated me all along the project, knowing my dedication to the subject and thought I am more than able to complete this project: Dr. Marsha Gordon, Dr. Lavern A. Wright, Dr. Lester Reid, Rahim Samuel Mama, Pastor Roland Dalo, Yanick Gil, and Jerry Izouele.

And last but not least, thank you to all the original readers of this book when it was in its infancy. Without your enthusiasm and encouragement, this book may have never been ready.

Contents

Acronyms

BJR	Best Judgment Rule
CAPEX	Capital Expenditures
CDO	Collateral Debt Obligations
CSR	Corporate Social Responsibility
Del. Ch	Delaware Chancery Court
DGCL	Delaware General Corporation Law
DCF	Discounted cash Flow
EBITDA	Earnings before Interest, Tax, Depreciation and Amortization
EU	European Union
EV	Enterprise Value
GAO	Governmental Accountability Office
IPO	Initial Purchase Offer
LBO	leveraged Buyout
LOI	Letter of Intent
MAC	Material Adverse Change
MAE	Material Adverse Effect
M&A	Mergers and Acquisitions
MBO	Management buyout
NOL	Net Operating Loss
S&P	Standard & Poor
US	United States
WACC	Weighted Average Cost of Capital

List of Cited Cases

In Martin Marietta Materials, Inc. v. Vulcan Materials Co., No. 7102-CS (Del. Ch. May 4, 2012).

Titan Investment Fund II, LP v. Freedom Mortgage Corp.

Siga Technologies, Inc. v. PharmAthene 132 A.3d 1108 (Del. 2015)

Gillenardo v. Connor Broad. Del. Co., 2002 WL 991110, at *1 (Del. Super. Apr. 30, 2002).

Williams Cos. v. Energy Transfer Equity, 159 A.3d 264 (Del. 2017).

Akorn, *Inc. v.* Fresenius Kabi *AG, 198 A. 3d 724-2018* (Del. 2018).

Williams Cos. v. Energyfer Equity, 159 A.3d 264 (Del. 2017).

Moleney v. Brincat, 722 A. 2d 5, 10 (Del. 1998).

Francis v. New Jersey Bank, 432 A. 2d 814 (N. J. 1981).

In Re Walt Disney Co. Derivative Litigation, Del. Ch. 2003.

Brehm v. Eisner, 906 A.2d 27, 64 (Del. 2006).

Brehm v. Eisner, 906 A.2d 27, 64 (Del. 2006).

Malone v. Brincat , 722 A.2d 5 (Del. 1998).

Unocal Corp. v. Mesa Petroleum Co., 493 A. 2d. 946 (Del. 1985).

Smith v. Van Gorkhom, 488 A. 2d 858 (Del. 1985).

Revlon Inc., v. MacAndrews & Forbes Holding Inc., 506 A. 2d 173 (Del. 1985).

Paramount Communications, Inc. v. QVC Network, Inc. 637 A. 2d (Del. 1994).

Phelps Dodge v. Cyprus Amax Minerals Co., C.A N0. 17398 (Del. Ch. Sept. 27, 1999).

Mills Acquisition co. v. Macmillan, Inc., 559 A 2d. 1261 (Del. 1989).

Omnicare3 v. NCS Healthcare Inc., 818 A 2d. 914 (Del. 2003).

In Re Emerging Communications Shareholders Litigation, (Del. Ch., May 3, 2004).

In Re Citigroup, Inc., (Del. Ch. 2009).

Moran v. Household International Inc., 500 A. 2d 1346 (Del. 1985).

Versata Enterprises v. Selectica, Inc. (Del. 2010).

Air Prods & Chemicals, Inc., Airgas, Inc., (Del.Ch. Feb. 15, 2011.

Lipton v. News Int'l, Plc, 514 A.2d 1075, 1079 (Del. 1986).

Stephen A. Radin, The Business Judgment Rule 3612 (6th ed. 2009) (quoting Midland Food Servs., LLC v. Castle Hill Hldgs. V, LLC, 792 A.2d 920, 931 (Del. Ch.1999) (Strine, V. C.)).

Cochran v. Stifel Fin. Corp., 2000 WL 286722, at *10 n.41 (Del. Ch. Mar. 8, 2000) (Strine, V. C.), rev'd in part on other grounds, 809 A.2d 555 (Del. 2002).

Ct. Ch. R. 56 (c).

XI Specialty Ins. Co. v. WMI Liquidating Trust, 93 A.3d 1208, 1217 (Del. 2014).

Moran v. Household Int'l, Inc., 490 A.2d 1059, 1072 (Del. Ch. 1985).

KLM Royal Dutch Airlines v. Checchi, 698 A.2d 380 (Del. Ch. 1997).

Carmody v. Toll Brothers, Inc., 723 A.2d 1180 (Del. Ch. 1998).

Pontiac General Employees Retirement System v. Ballantine, C.A. No. 9789-VCL at *72–77 (Del. Ch. Oct. 14, 2014).

Malone v. Brincat, 722 A.2d 5, 12 (Del. 1998).

TSC Indus., Inc. v. Northway, Inc., 426 U.S. 438, 449 (1976).

In re Dollar Thrifty S'holder Litig., 14 A.3d 573, 598 (Del. Ch. 2010).

Ams. Mining Corp. v. Theriault, 51 A.3d 1213, 1239 (Del. 2012).

Weinberger v. UOP, Inc., 457 A.2d 701, 710 (Del. 1983).

Strassburger v. Earley, 752 A.2d 557, 581 (Del. Ch. 2000).

Duncan v. TheraTx, Inc., 775 A.2d 1019, 1023 (Del. 2000).

Ala. By-Prods. Corp. v. Neal, 588 A.2d 255, 256 (Del. 1991).

M.G. Bancorporation, Inc. v. LeBeau, 737 A.2d 513, 520 (Del. 1999).

In William Richard Kruse v. Synapse Wireless, Inc., C. A. No. 12392-VCS (Del. Ch. July 14, 2020).

Hoyd v. Trussway Holdings LLC, 2019 WL 994048 (Del Ch. Feb. 28, 2019).

In re Appraisal of DFC Global Corp., 2016 Del. Ch. LEXIS 103 (Del. Ch. July 8, 2016).

In re Appraisal of Columbia Pipeline Group, Inc., 2019 WL 3778370 (Del. Ch. Aug. 12, 2019).

In re Appraisal of Jarden Corp., 2019 WL 3244085 (Del. Ch. July 19, 2019).

In re Appraisal of Stillwater Mining Co., 2019 WL 3943851 (Del. Ch. Aug. 21, 2019).

In Berger v. Pubco Corp., No. 509, 208 (Del., July 9, 2009).

In Re United Capital Corp, (Consolidated Stockholders Litigation) C.A. No. 11619-VCMR.

In Rudd v. Brown, et al, C.A. No. 2019-0775 MTZ (Del. Ch. Sept. 11, 2020).

In re United Capital Corp., Stockholders Litigation, C.A. No. 11619-VCMR (Del. Ch. Jan. 4, 2017).

In MTA Can. Royalty Corp. v. Compania Minera Pangea, S.A. De C.V., No. N19C-11-228 AML CCLD, 2020 Del. Super. LEXIS 2780 (Sept. 16, 2020).

CHAPTER 1

Overview of Mergers and Acquisitions

1.1 General

Mergers and acquisitions (M&A) is a general term that describes the consolidation of companies or assets through various types of financial transactions, including mergers, acquisitions, consolidations, tender offers, purchase of assets, and management acquisitions. Mergers and acquisitions take place for many strategic business reasons, but the most common reasons for any business combination are economic at their core.

1.2 Cross-Border M&A Trends

Cross-border M&A sales in developed countries declined by 40 percent in 2019, to $411 billion. Amid sluggish Eurozone growth and Brexit, European M&A sales halved to $190 billion. Deals targeting U.S. companies, at $157 billion, remained significant—accounting for 32 percent of the value of total cross-border M&As. In developing and transition economies, net M&A sales declined by 37 percent, to $80 billion. The decline of cross-border M&As in 2019 was much stronger than the 14 percent decrease in total M&A activity (including domestic deals) worldwide, continuing the trend of the last few years in the relative unpopularity of cross-border expansions and consolidations through deals. The fall in global cross-border M&As sales was deepest in the services sector, followed by the manufacturing sector.

F. Lessambo, *U.S. Mergers and Acquisitions*,
https://doi.org/10.1007/978-3-030-85735-6_1

In the primary sector, the largest deal was the acquisition of gold mining company Goldcorp (Canada) by Newmont (U.S.) for $9.9 billion. In manufacturing, net M&A sales targeting chemical and chemical products returned to prior values, at $35 billion, after large megadeals in 2018 ($119 billion). In contrast, the value of deals in the pharmaceutical industry almost doubled, to $98 billion. This included the largest deal recorded in any industry in 2019, in which Takeda (Japan) acquired the share capital of Shire (Ireland) for $60 billion. In services, net cross-border M&A sales fell by 54 percent to $215 billion. The largest divestment in 2019 was a $36 billion IPO of Myriad, an affiliate of Naspers (South Africa) in the Netherlands.

1.3 Methods of Business Combination

There are several methods for achieving a business combination. It is useful to have an understanding of these different methods. Hereafter, the term acquisitions will be used to refer to any type of business combination.

- Acquisition

An acquisition usually refers to the purchase of the assets of a company. However, in the remainder of this course, the term will be used in a much broader sense to indicate the purchase of shares, assets, or companies in the merger process. Thus, the narrow, distinct meaning of the term will not be used. An acquisition can take the form of a purchase of the stock or other equity interests of the target entity, or the acquisition of all or a substantial amount of its assets. Share purchases—in a share purchase the buyer buys the shares of the target company from the shareholders of the target company. The buyer will take on the company with all its assets and liabilities. Asset purchases—in an asset purchase the buyer buys the assets of the target company from the target company. In simplest form, this leaves the target company as an empty shell, and the cash it receives from the acquisition is then paid back to its shareholders by dividend or through liquidation. However, one of the advantages of an asset purchase for the buyer is that it can "cherry-pick" the assets that it wants and leave the assets—and liabilities—that it does not.

- Merger

In a merger, two separate companies combine and only one of them survives. In other words, the merged (acquired) company goes out of existence, leaving its assets and liabilities to the acquiring company. Usually when two companies of significantly different sizes merge, the smaller company will merge into the larger one, leaving the larger company intact.

- Consolidation

A consolidation is a combination of two or more companies in which an entirely new corporation is formed and all merging companies cease to exist. Shares of the new company are exchanged for shares of the merging ones. Two similarly sized companies usually consolidate rather than merge. Although the distinction between merger and consolidation is important, the terms are often used interchangeably, with either used to refer generally to a joining of the assets and liabilities of two companies.

- Leveraged Buyout

A leveraged buyout (LBO) is a type of acquisition that occurs when a group of investors, sometimes led by the management of a company (management buyout or MBO), borrows funds to purchase the company. The assets and future earnings of the company are used to secure the financing required to purchase the company. Sometimes employees are allowed to participate through an employee stock ownership plan, which may provide tax advantages and improve employee productivity by giving employees an equity stake in the company.

- Holding Company

A holding company is a company that owns sufficient voting stock to have a controlling interest in one or more companies called subsidiaries. Effective working control or substantial influence can be gained through ownership of as little as 5 percent to as much as 51 percent of the outstanding shares, depending on how widely the shares are distributed.

A holding company that engages in the management of the subsidiaries is called a parent company.

- Divestitures

While divestitures do not represent a business combination, they are a means of facilitating the acquisition of part of a company. Sometimes divestitures are used by companies as a means to improve earnings and shareholder value or as a means of raising capital. A divestiture involves the sale of a portion of a company. Two popular means of divestiture are spin-offs and equity carve-outs.

In a spin-off, a company distributes all of its shares in a subsidiary to the company's shareholders as a tax-free exchange. The reorganization of AT&T is an example of a spin-off. AT&T was reorganized into three separate publicly traded corporations, and a fourth business was sold. What remained was AT&T, comprised of long distance and wireless phone businesses, a credit card business, and two other companies that were formed and spun off to shareholders by giving them stock in the two companies. One of these companies, now Lucent Technologies, was an equipment producer and research company. It was spun-off to avoid conflicts with customers of other AT&T products. The other company was NCR, a computer company. This was spun-off to remove the effects of a poor-performing business from AT&T's results. An equity carve-out is similar to a spin-off. It occurs when a company sells some of its shares in a subsidiary to the public. This raises additional capital for the company.

- Hostile versus Friendly Combinations

Acquisitions may be hostile or friendly. In a hostile acquisition, the acquiring, or bidder, company makes an offer to purchase the acquired or target company, but the management of the target company resists the offer. At that point, the bidder often tries to take control of the target through a tender offer, whereby the bidder offers to purchase a majority of the target's stock at a predetermined price, set sufficiently higher than the current market price to attract the shareholders' attention. Hostile acquisitions are typically more expensive for both parties since they involve more time and negotiations, fees to experts such as attorneys and investment bankers, and may result in a bidding war where multiple bidders enter the contest for control. The large number of hostile acquisitions in the 1980s led to the coining of the term "market for corporate control." This terminology reflects the view that acquisitions are market-based contests whereby corporate managers bid to control corporate assets, with the highest bidder receiving control. Even though hostile acquisitions receive much of the media attention surrounding acquisitions, the great majority of acquisitions are; friendly. In a friendly acquisition, the management of both companies come to an agreement over the terms of the acquisition. Many acquisitions that begin as hostile end up being completed on a friendly basis.

1.4 Motives for Acquisitions

The overriding motive for any acquisition should be to maximize shareholder value. There has been increasing emphasis on maximizing shareholder value and managers are under more and more pressure to do so. The threat of a hostile takeover places pressures on all corporate managers to manage their companies to maximize value or risk being taken over and restructured by another management. Increasingly competitive global capital markets, active institutional investors, active and independent boards of directors, and better informed market participants have all led to an increased focus by shareholders on shareholder value, and have placed increased pressure on corporate managers to maximize shareholder value.

Acquisitions are a means of creating shareholder value by exploiting synergies, increasing growth, replacing inefficient managers, gaining market power, and extracting benefits from financial and operational restructuring. However, for value to be created, the benefits of these motives must exceed the costs.

These motives are considered to add shareholder value:

- Economies of scale: This refers to the fact that the combined company can often reduce duplicate departments or operations, lowering the costs of the company relative to theoretically the same revenue stream, thus increasing profit.
- Increased revenue/Increased Market Share: This motive assumes that the company will be absorbing a major competitor and its power (by capturing increased market share) to set prices.
- Cross selling: For example, a bank buying a stockbroker could then sell its banking products to the stockbroker's customers, while the

broker can sign up the bank's customers for brokerage accounts. On the other hand, a manufacturer can acquire and sell complementary products.

- Synergy: Better use of complementary resources.
- Taxes: A profitable company can buy a loss maker to use the target's tax write-offs. In the U.S. and many other countries, rules are in place to limit the ability of profitable companies to "shop" for loss making companies, limiting the tax motive of an acquiring company.
- Geographical or other diversification: This is designed to smooth the earnings results of a company, which over the long term smoothens the stock price of a company, giving conservative investors more confidence in investing in the company. However, this does not always deliver value to shareholders (see below).
- Resource transfer: Resources are unevenly distributed across firms and the interaction of target and acquiring firm resources can create value through either by overcoming information asymmetry or by combining scarce resources.
- Financial restructuring: A change in control can lead to a more cost-effective or safer capital structure, and more efficient use of financial assets.
- Business mix restructuring: The acquirer may divest non-core businesses.

The following motives are considered to not add shareholder value:

- Diversification: While this may hedge a company against a downturn in an individual industry, it fails to deliver value, since it is possible for individual shareholders to achieve the same hedge by diversifying their portfolios at a much lower cost than those associated with a merger.
- Overextension: Tend to make the organization fuzzy and unmanageable.
- Manager's hubris: manager's overconfidence about expected synergies from M&A, which results in overpayment for the target company.
- Empire Building. Managers have larger companies to manage and hence more power.

- Manager's Compensation: In the past, certain executive management teams had their payout based on the total amount of profit of the company, instead of the profit per share, which would give the team a perverse incentive to buy companies to increase the total profit while decreasing the profit per share (which hurts the owners of the company, the shareholders), although some empirical studies show that compensation is rather linked to profitability and not mere profits of the company.
- Bootstrapping: Example: How ITT executed its merger.
- Vertical integration: Companies acquire part of a supply chain and benefit from the resources.

1.5 Growth Through Acquisitions

There are numerous reasons for a company to want to grow. Growth is often considered vital to the health of a company. A stagnating company may have difficulty attracting high-quality management. Furthermore, larger companies may pay higher salaries to top management than smaller companies. In some industries, size itself may bring competitive advantages. For example, marketing dominance may be strengthened through improved access to advertising. In addition, a large company may have significantly higher production or distribution efficiencies than a smaller one. Sometimes growth is a means of survival. For example, companies in the telecommunications industry have grown through acquisition in an effort to compete to control phone lines, cable systems, and content. The merger of Viacom, Blockbuster, and Paramount created a conglomeration of television and movie production, video distribution and publishing, and cable channels in an industry where many companies are merging to compete to become comprehensive media powerhouses. Firms in the defense industry have merged to survive in a declining market. Finally, tax laws may encourage merger growth.

Despite these reasons to grow, growth by itself does not necessarily benefit either the stockholders or the managers of a company. Growth is not something that must be achieved regardless of its price. Throughout this course, emphasis will be placed on an acquisition's impact on value. Careful comparisons between benefits and costs will be made. A good acquisition will be defined as one that can be expected to increase the stock price (other things being equal) of the acquiring company.

Furthermore, a merger is not always the best way to grow. A company can achieve internal expansion through investment in projects generated within the company itself. By doing so, efficiency may be improved, existing activities may be expanded, and new products may be introduced.

External expansion takes place through an acquisition. Because of the similarities between the acquisition and the capital budgeting process, the same approval and review forms, control procedures, and post-audit examinations commonly used for analyzing capital expenditures can be applied to an acquisition analysis as well. In addition, consideration should be given at the highest levels of the business to how the proposed acquisition fits in with the needs and strategic thrust of the company. With a good fit, even at a relatively high price, the company being considered may be viewed as a good investment. Without a good fit, the acquisition may not be a good deal at almost any price.

1.6 Financial Analysis

An acquisition is essentially as an investment decision. An initial outlay is invested to obtain expected future benefits. A good acquisition will generate greater benefits, in present value terms, than its costs. The likely effect of a good acquisition will be to increase the stock value of the acquiring company. To properly conduct this type of acquisition analysis, some strategic concepts and many valuation tools are required. The discipline of corporate finance shapes both the strategic and the financial analysis necessary to identify and evaluate acquisition candidates and assess the impact of acquisitions on company value.

Acquisitions are financial decisions that should be consistent with the company's goal of shareholder wealth maximization. Sound and thorough financial analysis should be a part of any acquisition. Many acquisitions that fail, in the sense that they do not add value to the acquiring company, do so because they were motivated by wishful thinking rather than sound and thorough financial analysis. This discipline starts with the methods for analyzing a company's financial statements. The next step is an understanding of lenders' and investors' required returns and corporate valuation analysis. Through this framework, the financial analyst will be better able to view the acquisition process as a competition with other stock purchasers, all of whom are looking for good buys.

Acquisitions are also strategic decisions that should be consistent with the mission of the acquiring company and fit into its overall strategic plan. The reasons for an acquisition must be understood in the context of a company's strategic analysis. Acquisitions can be justified in terms of the competitive advantages they produce (e.g., marketing positions may be strengthened or production costs reduced). Other motives include improved management, tax benefits, or defensive maneuvers to prevent takeover by other companies. Finally, many acquisitions produce benefits purely from the financial and business restructuring that follows a change in control—as illustrated by the value increases following leveraged buyouts.

1.7 Accounting for Mergers

Two methods of accounting for acquisitions—purchase and pooling of interests—are often discussed. Financial statements that record the results of an acquisition must follow one of these two techniques. Financial managers must be aware of the accounting requirements as merger negotiations near completion.

Under the purchase method, the acquiring company as an investment, analogous to a capital budgeting expenditure, treats the acquired company. A totally new ownership is assumed. Asset values are reappraised in light of estimates of their current market values, and the balance sheet is restated to the new levels. Because of these adjustments, goodwill often results. Goodwill is the amount by which the price paid for a company exceeds the company's estimated net worth at market value. Goodwill must be written off against future net income over a reasonable period. Such deductions against income are deductible for tax purposes in most countries.

Under the pooling of interest's method, the assets and liabilities of the two combining companies are simply added together. Since only the book values of the assets and liabilities are considered, no goodwill results. In most countries, there are severe restrictions on a company's use of the pooling of interest's method. Because of these restrictions, the pooling of interest's method is used much less today than it was in the past.

1.8 Mergers Negotiation and Due Diligence

Negotiating the merger can be difficult. The simple answer to making it work to hire the best advisors. Their job is to manage the negotiation process in such a way that it reaches a satisfactory conclusion—both parties must see a gain, and both parties must be protected—and it does not conflict with legal and regulatory constraints. The goal is to reach an agreement that is embodied in the "sale and purchase agreement"—which includes all the key terms of the deal, such as price, payment method, adjustments, constraints on the seller as well as accounting definitions, accounting and tax warranties and indemnities.

Quite often, a proposed merger or acquisition gets canned or valued down following conflicts over intellectual property rights, personnel, accounting discrepancies, or incompatibilities in integrating information technology systems. The process of researching, understanding and, in some cases, avoiding these risks is known as due diligence.

"Due diligence is going in and digging a hole in the ground and seeing if there's oil, instead of taking someone's word on it," says Joseph Bankoff, a lawyer. "If you don't do a sufficient amount of due diligence, you don't really know what questions to ask."

Due diligence for mergers and acquisitions requires broad and deep data analysis of assets and liabilities, including large balance sheet items such as accounts receivable, inventory, and accounts payable to establish fair market value. It also means analyzing collections of receivables and inventory to identify doubtful accounts or obsolete stock, and analyzing cash receipts and billing files using historical trends to assess the reliability and adequacy of projected cash flows. The due diligence team must sift through press reports and regulatory filings to uncover any actual or potential legal, environmental, or other problems. In the case of a technology acquisition, a due diligence investigation should answer pertinent questions such as whether an application is too bulky to run on the mobile devices the marketing plan calls for or whether customers are right when they complain about a lack of scalability for a high-end system.

< > Due diligence entails taking all the "reasonable steps" to ensure that both buyer and seller get what they expect "and not a lot of other things that you did not count on or expect," Bankoff explains. The process involves everything from reading the fine print in corporate legal and financial documents such as equity vesting plans and patents to interviewing customers, corporate officers, and key developers. It helps to identify potential risks and red flags.

1.9 Financing the Deal

Mergers are generally differentiated from acquisitions partly by the way in which they are financed and partly by the relative size of the companies. Various methods of financing an M&A deal exist:

A company acquiring another will frequently pay for the other company with cash. Such transactions are usually termed acquisitions rather than mergers because the shareholders of the target company are removed from the picture and the target comes under the (indirect) control of the bidder's shareholders alone. An acquisition can involve a cash and debt combination, or a combination of cash and stock of the purchasing entity, or just stock.

A "merger" or "merger of equals" is often financed by all stock deal (a stock swap), known in the UK as an all share deal. Such deals are considered a merger rather than acquisitions because neither company pays money and the shareholders of each company end up as the combined shareholders of the merged company. There are two methods of merging companies in this way:

- one company takes ownership of the other, issuing new shares in itself to the shareholders of the company being acquired as payment or
- a third company is created which takes ownership of both companies (or their assets) in exchange for shares in itself issued to the shareholders of the two merging companies.

Where one company is notably larger than the other, people may nevertheless be wary of calling the deal a merger, as the shareholders of the larger company will still dominate the merged company.

If cash is paid, the cash can be raised in a number of ways. The company may have sufficient cash available in its account, but this is unlikely. More often, the cash will be borrowed from a bank, or raised by an issue of bonds, or of equity. Acquisitions financed through debt are known as leveraged buyouts, and the debt will typically be moved down onto the balance sheet of the acquired company. Many leveraged acquisitions include a component of mezzanine debt, which falls between senior secured bank debt and equity.

1.10 Post-Merger Integration

Some problems must inevitably occur when two companies combine; however, these problems can be anticipated and minimized. Managers of the acquired company will feel some loss of autonomy since their decisions must now be meshed with the policies of the merged company. Once-simple procedures become complicated by a new control system. Furthermore, the acquired company's managers are often concerned about personal recognition, advancement, and job security in the new company. Historically, many managers of acquired companies have lost their jobs following an acquisition.

Problems in the acquiring company will emerge as well. Its strengths and weaknesses and the skills and potential of its personnel will not be immediately apparent in the combined company. In addition, the staff of the acquiring company may lack the expertise to understand completely the production processes of the acquired company and may therefore be unable to make appropriate decisions about them. Disciplines, procedures, and controls that have been well established over time may not work as well in the new environment. There may be a clash of corporate cultures.

1.11 Cultural issues Cultural in a Merger

Corporate culture is the manner in which a company does its business. It begins with the general concept of how the senior management team wants to operate the business and percolates down through the organization in the form of management structure, how decisions are made, policies and procedures, the types of people hired, and even its marketing efforts.

Examples of the opposite extremes of corporate culture are:

- Command-and-control. Senior management makes all key decisions and restricts the flow of information to people lower in the organization. The organizational structure is strongly hierarchical. This culture typically uses close adherence to the annual budget as a "carrot and stick" method for rewarding managers.
- Localized responsibility. The senior management team is in charge of strategy and shifts all tactical decision-making lower in the organization. There is broad distribution of information throughout the

organization. There tends to be more emphasis on an upgraded work environment, in order to spur productivity and reduce employee turnover.

- There can be serious problems with an acquisition if the corporate culture of the acquirer is of the command-and-control variety and the target company practices localized responsibility. The typical result is a large initial surge in employee turnover. If the reverse situation arises, employees of the target company will not be used to having responsibility thrust upon them, which can result in a prolonged period of confusion, reduced operating results, and employee turnover. In short, it is difficult to mix these two extreme forms of corporate culture, and so the due diligence team should estimate the impact of the acquirer's culture on the target company.
- The dichotomy just noted was for the two extreme forms of corporate culture. In reality, most organizations fall somewhere between these extremes, so the amount of cultural conflict is likely to be reduced. Nonetheless, there will be conflicts, which the due diligence team should highlight in its report to senior management. Seemingly, trivial issues that the team should take note of include any differences from the acquirer's culture concerning such issues as:

  - Community involvement
  - Dress code
  - Flexible work hours
  - Matching of contributions to non-profit entities
  - Political activity
  - Special events for employees.

Another culture issue that is potentially serious is the presence of any illegal activities. They could take the form of misstatement of the financial statements, outright theft of assets, the routine circumvention of accounting policies, and so forth. If there is evidence of such activities, it is entirely possible that the attitude of the management team is allowing it to occur throughout the business. For example, they may be ignoring the theft of assets by the family of the owner or have imposed such difficult goals that employees can only achieve them by committing fraud. This type of environment is usually a clear indicator to an acquirer to terminate its pursuit of the business and go elsewhere.

CHAPTER 2

Legal Framework

2.1 General

Generally, the statutory law of the state in which the target corporation or other business entity is formed governs many important aspects of the affairs of such entity, including with respect to mergers and acquisitions. State statutory laws set up the requirements that must be satisfied for target corporations to validly enter into and consummate mergers and acquisitions. Whenever statutory laws are silent, common laws kick in to supply rules and principles that affect acquisition M&A. For instance, the common understanding is that the directors of the target corporation acts in good faith, on an informed basis and in the best interests of stockholders. Because most corporations and other business entities are incorporated in the State of Delaware, the Delaware Corporate Laws are deemed the applicable laws in several M&A.

2.2 Letter of Engagement

As a rule, the statutory law of the state in which the target corporation or other business entity is formed governs many important aspects of the affairs of such entity, including with respect to mergers and acquisitions. State statutory laws set up the requirements that must be satisfied for target corporations to validly enter into and consummate mergers and acquisitions. Whenever statutory laws are silent, common laws kick in

F. Lessambo, *U.S. Mergers and Acquisitions*,
https://doi.org/10.1007/978-3-030-85735-6_2

to supply rules and principles that affect acquisition M&A. For instance, the common understanding is that the directors of the target corporation acts in good faith, on an informed basis, and in the best interests of stockholders. Because most corporations and other business entities are incorporated in the State of Delaware, the Delaware Corporate Laws are deemed the applicable laws in several M&A.

2.3 Confidentiality Agreement

Having a separate confidentiality agreement gives the parties the flexibility to conduct due diligence of certain nonpublic information before negotiating a term sheet or letter of intent. In other words, it provides the parties with written protection in the event of disclosure of confidential information prior to entering into a term sheet or letter of intent. The negotiation of confidentiality agreements tends to center around a few key issues that the target company has heightened concerns with strategic buyers. For instance, the target company may want to prohibit potential buyers from contacting its employees, suppliers, and customers without advance consent. In general, the confidentiality agreement provides that its employees and agents would hold the buyer responsible for any breach of the confidentiality agreement, and that such employees and agents must be informed about the confidential nature of the information before being provided any information. An important issue when negotiating a confidentiality agreement is the duration of its restrictions. A period of 18–24 months is common. Besides monetary damages in case of breach, most confidentiality agreements allow the target to obtain injunctive relief (specific performance) in addition to any other remedies available at law or equity (monetary damages). For instance, in Martin Marietta, Inc., the Chancery Court concluded that Martin Marietta breached the confidentiality agreements by using confidential information in determining whether to launch a hostile bid and disclosing extensive details regarding the confidential merger discussions and other confidential information in its securities filings and other communications.[1]

2.4 The Term Sheet

The Term Sheet is a non-binding expression of interest by a buyer that outlines the price and structure of a transaction. The term sheet serves as a template and basis for more detailed, legally binding documents.

Its function is to determine if the parties agree on the price and structure of the transaction before both parties invest significant time and money on professional fees. Put differently, a term sheet is not a contract or a binding agreement but just an expression of a possible business transaction between the Target and the Buyer. No party is bound for a transaction until and unless the parties to this transaction execute definitive agreements. A term sheet summarizes the main points of the deal agreements and sorts out the differences before actually executing the legal agreements and starting with the time-consuming due diligence. The contents and clauses of the term sheet vary from transaction to transaction. However, the Delaware Courts, in several decisions held that a letter agreement and term sheet created an enforceable obligation that the parties negotiate a credit facility agreement in good faith.[2]

In SIGA Technologies v. PharmeAthene,[3] the Supreme Court of Delaware found that SIGA disregarded the term-sheet terms and attempted to negotiate a definitive license agreement that contained economic and other terms drastically different and significantly more favorable to SIGA than those in the term sheet (LATS). Therefore, the Court held that:

> Where parties agree to negotiate in good faith in accordance with a term sheet, that obligation to negotiate in good faith is enforceable.

It is worthy to note that under Delaware law, bad faith is not simply bad judgment or negligence, but rather it implies the conscious doing of a wrong because of dishonest purpose or moral obliquity. Bad faith is different from the negative idea of negligence in that it contemplates a state of mind affirmatively operating with furtive design or ill will.

2.5 The Letter of Intent

Similar to the Term Sheet, the LOI will specify the terms of the transaction, but in detail. A letter of intent is a document declaring the preliminary commitment of one party to do business with another. The letter outlines the chief terms of a prospective deal and is commonly used in business transactions. Its purpose is to establish milestones for the transaction as well as encourage the parties to complete due diligence, accelerate negotiations of the definitive agreement. A letter of Intent would include not only the amount that the buyer proposes to pay for the acquired business but also a great amount of details as to the form of payment (i.e., cash, stock of the buyer, seller note, a combination of these). In addition, the timing and manner of payment is usually specified to describe how much will be paid at closing versus following the closing, and whether any post-closing payments will be contingent upon future events or on the business meeting certain performance targets or other metrics. If the buyer expects a portion of the purchase price to be placed in escrow to secure any indemnification or other obligations of the seller, such provisions would be inserted as well. More, the letter of intent includes some binding terms such as exclusivity for the bidder. In Gillenardo v. Connor Broadcasting Delaware Co., a Superior Court judge considered a letter of intent setting forth the potential purchase price and other financing and negotiating terms for a sale of two radio stations, including an attached draft of the purchase agreement and related exhibits.[4]

2.6 Merger Contract

After the transaction, structure has been determined, the other terms and conditions of the transaction will need to be negotiated and materialized in a definitive acquisition agreement. Although US acquisition agreements vary in many respects, most will share the same basic components, including the following:

2.6.1 The Offer and the Merger

The purchase price may have a variable aspect or measure used to adjust the payment to be made by the buyer. Sellers also should consider other factors that may affect cash received at closing such as taxes and contingent payments, such as escrows, earn-outs, and seller notes. Most deals include a purchase price mechanism that adjusts the purchase price for events that cannot be measured until after the deal closes.

- Escrow

In M&A transactions, an escrow provision is used to insure that the seller meets certain conditions before an agreed amount of funds is released to the seller. ...Escrows are held for some period to protect the buyers of a business against any unforeseen financial losses after the closing. To recover funds from the escrow account, the buyer must assert a claim for indemnification or other recovery under the acquisition agreement, and if undisputed by the seller, the escrow agent releases from escrow the amount of such claim to the buyer. If the seller disputes the claim, the escrow agent retains the amount of the pending claim in escrow until the resolution of the dispute, by settlement, litigation, or arbitration. If no claims are outstanding upon the termination date of an escrow arrangement, the remaining amount in escrow is distributed to the seller.

- Holdback

A holdback is a mechanism used by purchasers to withhold payment of a portion of the purchase price until some post-closing condition has been satisfied. Put differently, it is simply a covenant by the purchaser to make payment of the withheld amount(s) upon satisfaction of the release conditions. In some cases, the purchaser will deliver a promissory note; in others, the parties simply rely on the covenant in the acquisition agreement. Holdback arrangements reduce the risk that selling parties transfer the sale proceeds to jurisdictions where enforcement of claims for recovery may be impracticable or impossible. They also guard against the transfer of sale proceeds to persons or entities against whom enforcement of claims for recovery may otherwise be difficult.

- Earn-outs

An earn-out is a provision in a definitive agreement, generally an asset transaction, providing the seller's shareholders with the right to receive additional consideration after closing if the company's earnings over a specified period meet certain thresholds, or more precisely, targets (metrics). Earn-outs can be a useful tool for buyers and sellers with different views on the value of the business, allowing them to avoid difficult purchase price negotiations. In order to accurately gauge performance against earn-out measures, it is necessary to isolate the target business from the other businesses of the buyer. Sellers often attempt to vest target management with significant control of and discretion over the continued operation of the target business for some period after the closing, which can inhibit the integration of the target business into the corporate organization of the buyer. Typical performance measures for earn-outs include target company pre-tax earnings, Earnings Before Interests, Tax, Depreciations, and Amortizations (EBITDA), and gross revenues. The general view is that earn-outs based on gross revenues are less subject to manipulation by the buyer. Earn-out payments can also be based on the attainment of non- financial milestones, such as the successful development or regulatory approval of new products. The typical length of an earn-out arrangement is between one and five years, although performance is at times measured and payments made on an annual or other basis.

2.6.2 *Representations and Warranties*

In a M&A deal, each party to a purchase agreement makes certain representations and warranties that serve to allocate risk between the parties and provide a basis for post-closing indemnification obligations. A representation is an assertion as to a fact, true on the date the representation is made, that is given to induce another party to enter into a contract or take some other action. A warranty is a promise that the assertion of existing fact or future facts are or will be true, along with an implied promise of indemnity if the assertion is false. In M&A transactions, representations and warranties are given by both parties to disclose material information. A seller's representations and warranties serve several purposes: (i) they give important information about the stock or assets being sold, (ii) provide a basis for the buyer's right to terminate before or at closing, and (iii) affect the buyer's right to indemnification by the seller and/or its principals. Standard representations relate to due organization, valid existence and good standing, power and authority to operate the business and to enter into the agreement, and compliance with laws. Other representations and warranties relate to the subject matter of the agreement, such as title to assets, liens and encumbrances, intellectual property rights, taxes, and litigation. In practice, a seller would attempt to limit representations and warranties to apply only to things and matters that are "material" and to add "knowledge" standards to limit the statement of fact to things that the seller actually knows of or should have known of. Conversely, a buyer wants the seller's representations and warranties to be unqualified and as broad as possible. A breach or inaccuracy of a representation or warranty can also provide the other party with a right to terminate or refuse to close the transaction.

2.6.3 Covenants

Basically, a covenant in a definitive agreement is a promise by one or both of the parties to the transaction to do or not do something either before the closing or occasionally after. For example, the target covenants not to make any material changes to its business between the execution of the definitive agreement and the closing. If you look at a standard definitive agreement-they generally follow the same format for meaningful transactions-you will see separate sections for closing conditions, covenants, and representations and warranties. While they have common aspects, they are different terms which some lawyers have difficulty remembering. The remedies for violation of these provisions can include termination of the transaction and post-closing indemnification. Stated another way, they are important contractual provisions which can dramatically affect the transaction, and thus often are the subject of intense negotiations and should not be agreed to cavalierly.

Pre-Closing Covenants

Whenever there is a delay between the signing of the purchase agreement and the closing requirements of the transaction, then the purchase agreement would need to include certain pre-closing covenants. Most of the pre-closing covenants are made by the seller in favor of the buyer and are generally intended to give assurances to the buyer that there will be no surprises during the interim period or at closing. The buyer may also give the seller pre-closing covenants. These are usually limited to the buyer agreeing to obtain all applicable governmental and third-party approvals and consents and perhaps to secure financing to fund the purchase price. Below are the most common positive covenants and restrictive covenants made by the seller:

- The seller will continue to operate the business in the ordinary course and will not take any major actions without the prior consent of the buyer.

- The seller will agree to provide the buyer reasonable access to the seller's premises, personnel, and assets to allow the buyer to continue its due diligence.
- The seller will covenant to obtain all required governmental and third-party approvals and consents.
- The seller may agree to a "no shop" clause where the seller agrees not to enter into any competing negotiations with another buyer.

Post-Closing Covenants
In general, both parties to a M&A make a number of post-closing covenants. These include restrictive covenants made by the seller and owners in favor of the buyer regarding confidential information of the target, non-competition and non-solicitation of employees and customers for a limited number of years, and non-disparagement. In an asset deal, the buyer may agree, through positive covenant, to offer employment to each of the target's employees for at least the same compensation and benefits being paid by the seller. The parties will also agree on how taxes for the target will be filed and paid. If the transaction is an asset purchase, the parties will also agree on how the assets should be allocated for tax purposes. In general, the seller would prefer an allocation that emphasizes capital gain over ordinary income, while the buyer would go for an allocation that allows its business to maximize depreciation and amortization of the assets it is acquiring.

2.6.4 Conditions to Consummation of the Merger

In general, a merger agreement would specify that the merger be consummated when all of the conditions stipulated in the agreement are either satisfied or waived by the parties to the agreement.

2.6.5 Material Adverse Change (MAC) and Material Adverse Effect (MAE) Clauses

An MAE is broadly defined as any event that has, or would reasonably be expected to have, a material adverse effect on the target group's business, assets, financial condition, or results of operations, subject to certain carve-outs. It can also include the seller's inability to consummate the transaction. The Delaware courts, for instance, apply a very high bar to finding an MAE, requiring that it must be "material when viewed from the long-term perspective of a reasonable buyer" and result in a durationally significant reduction in the target's long-term earnings power. If a MAC or MAE occurs, the transaction may generally be abandoned without penalty, although the condition can always be waived. For that reason, the Delaware courts have a strong bias toward facilitating the closure of transactions that have been heavily negotiated.

2.6.6 Closing and Post-Closing Conditions

Any conditions contained in the definitive agreement, which must be satisfied or waived in order for the transaction to be consummated. For example, the buyer must raise the financing it needs toward the purchase price before the deal can close or the seller must execute any assignments for the buyer to obtain ownership of property, contracts, and the like. Not surprisingly, closings can be complicated with many documents and forms to be signed which places a premium on the deal lawyer's expertise, planning and organizational abilities. Closings can be nerve-racking experiences, but somehow they are done.

Most M&A transactions include post-closing conditions (e.g., purchase price adjustment). The most common is the earn-out, which requires the seller to calculate an estimated adjustment immediately prior to closing. In most adjustments, the buyer and its accountants prepare a detailed calculation of the post-closing adjustment and deliver it to the seller within a specified time after closing.

2.6.7 Indemnification

Indemnification provisions allow a party, usually the buyer, to recover damages for (i) breaches of the representations, warranties and covenants of the other party and (ii) liabilities that the indemnifying party (usually the seller in an asset purchase transaction) has agreed to retain. When a breach of the acquisition agreement occurs, in the absence of an indemnification provision, parties may have several remedies available, including asserting an action for breach of contract or a common law claim of fraud.

Limitations to Indemnification

In M&A deals, the final agreement contains the below limitations to the amount of the indemnification :

- Baskets/Deductibles

Baskets/deductibles are minimum thresholds that must be exceeded by the aggregate amount of all losses claimed by an indemnified party before it is entitled to receive an indemnification payment. Baskets/deductibles allow the target to avoid having to indemnify the buyer for relatively minor claims. Two types of thresholds then exist—a deductible and a tipping basket. When a deductible basket is agreed, only claims that exceed the agreed amount can be submitted (excess only). A level of the deductible is agreed. Only the claims that exceed the basket can be enforced. With a tipping basket, the total amount (first dollar) can be claimed once the total basket exceeds the agreed amount.

- De Minimis Amount

A materiality threshold is agreed for a de minimis clause. De minimis amount prevents an individual claim from being eligible for indemnification unless it exceeds a specified threshold amount, which is set at an amount below which the parties consider the claim a nuisance to deal with. This protects the vendor from the submission of many minor claims for compensation, which are immaterial compared to the agreed purchase price. At the same time, the de minimis clause helps to avoid a large number of legal disputes between the parties over minor amounts. De minimis thresholds are less common than baskets/deductibles and are frequently successfully resisted by buyers.

- Caps

A "cap" is the upper dollar limit of the seller's indemnification obligations to the buyer. It is the total amount of losses and damages a buyer is entitled to recover from the seller. In negotiating an indemnification cap, a seller will clearly seek the lowest cap possible, while a buyer will seek a high cap or no cap at all. Caps generally range between 10 and 25% of the purchase price, with such percentage often being higher in transactions with lower purchase prices. Recent market studies show that over half of all reported deals have caps of 10% or less of the total transaction value. The size of the cap often correlates to transaction size: almost

75% of the transactions having a cap in excess of 20% of total transaction value involve a transaction value of less than $75 million. In general, indemnification items excluded from the general cap are often subject to a secondary cap that is often equal to the purchase price.

Exceptions to Baskets and Caps

Caps and baskets only apply to unknown liabilities. If the buyer uncovers liabilities or issues prior to closing, those matters are usually excluded entirely from the caps and baskets. As such, the Buyer gets first-dollar protection against those liabilities or issues without limitation.

- Anti-Sandbagging

An anti-sandbagging provision prohibits the buyer from sandbagging or seeking post-closing recourse regarding matters which the buyer knew about at or prior to closing. It cut short any sandbagging provision, which may have stated that a buyer's remedies against the seller under the agreement are not impacted regardless of whether the buyer had knowledge, at or prior to closing, of the facts or circumstances giving rise to the claim. A typical anti-sandbagging provision may state:

The purchaser acknowledges that it has had the opportunity to conduct due diligence and investigation with respect to the Company, and in no event shall the seller have any liability to the Purchaser with respect to a breach of representation, warranty, or covenant under this Agreement to the extent that the Purchaser knew of such breach as of the Closing Date.

- Limitation periods

In addition to provisions concerning the level of liability, the liability of the vendor is also usually limited in terms of time (limitation periods). Care must be taken to ensure that longer periods of limitation or assessment periods apply in relation to tax claims. In practice, the period of the limitation of liability is normally between 18 and 36 months from the closing date, which is the date of completion of the purchase contract. In the case of violations of tax-related guarantees, depending on the country, liability may be customary for a period of up to six years from the closing date.

Indemnification Procedures

The indemnification section will include procedures for bringing indemnification claims and resolving disputes related thereto. For disputes involving third parties, the indemnifying party will usually seek to control the defense of the indemnification claim, as the indemnifying party will bear the cost and expense of an adverse ruling or decision. As such, promptly after receipt by an indemnified party of notice of the commencement of any Proceeding against it, such indemnified party will, if a claim is to be made against an indemnifying party under such, give notice to the indemnifying party of the commencement of such claim, but the failure to notify the indemnifying party will not relieve the indemnifying party of any liability that it may have to any indemnified party, except to the extent that the indemnifying party demonstrates that the defense of such action is prejudiced by the indemnifying party's failure to give such notice. However, if an indemnified party determines in good faith that there is a reasonable probability that a Proceeding may adversely affect it or its affiliates other than as a result of monetary damages for which it would be entitled to indemnification, the indemnified party may, by notice to the indemnifying party, assume the exclusive right to defend, compromise, or settle such Proceeding, but the indemnifying party will not be bound by any determination of a Proceeding so defended or any compromise or settlement effected without its consent. Nonetheless, with respect to any settlement that involves non-monetary relief affecting the indemnified party, the consent of the indemnified party is usually required.

2.7 Reasonable Best Effort Clause

The reasonable best efforts clause requires a party to take all reasonable steps to solve problems and consummate the transaction.[5] It is generally written as such:

> The parties shall use...reasonable best efforts to, and shall cause their respective Affiliates to use reasonable best efforts to, take, or cause to be taken, all actions, and to do, or cause to be done, and to assist and cooperate with the other parties in doing, all things necessary, proper, or advisable to consummate and make effect, in the most expeditious manner practicable, the merger.

2.8 Court Cases

It is behind the scope of this chapter to discuss all M&A clauses review under the Delaware Courts. Nonetheless, two selected clauses will be discussed: the MAE, and the Reasonable best effort clauses.

In Akorn v. Fresenius Kabi,[6] the Delaware Court of Chancery provided some guidance on quantitative benchmarks that are likely to influence future decisions: a 40% decline in earnings as indicative of a stand-alone MAE, and a 20% decline in valuation as indicative of an MAE in the bring-down condition. These benchmarks are not dispositive, and cases are fact-intensive and may turn on qualitative evidence. Vice Chancellor Laster found that Fresenius made the necessary showing to establish a general MAE. He also found the bring-down condition was not satisfied because the inaccuracy of Akorn's regulatory compliance representation constituted an MAE.

On appeal, the Supreme Court held that the record "adequately supports" the Court of Chancery's decision that Akorn had suffered a general MAE that excused any obligation to close by Fresenius. The Court found that the record "adequately supports" the Court of Chancery's determination that Fresenius properly terminated the merger based on a breach of regulatory representations and warranties that gave rise to an MAE, and that Fresenius itself had not engaged in a prior material breach of a covenant that would have prevented. More, the Court agreed with the Chancery Court findings did not breach its Reasonable Best Efforts Covenant and that its temporary breach of a so-called Hell-or-High-Water Covenant was not material. However, the Court declined to address whether Akorn breached the Ordinary Course Covenant and whether Fresenius was free to terminate the merger agreement for that additional reason, rather, it concluded that the issue whether Akorn breached the ordinary course covenant was irrelevant.

2.8.1 Williams Cos. V. Energyfer Equity[7]

Energy Transfer Equity, L.P. ("ETE"), a Delaware limited partnership, agreed to acquire the assets of The Williams Companies, Inc., ("Williams"), a Delaware corporation. The merger agreement contained, inter alia, a provision that required the parties to use "commercially reasonable efforts" to obtain the 721 opinion and to use "reasonable best efforts" to consummate the transaction.

The parties broadly agreed that they would use their reasonable best efforts to take, or cause to be taken, all actions, and to do, or cause to be done, and to assist and cooperate with the other parties in doing, all things necessary, proper or advisable to consummate and make effective, in the most expeditious manner practicable" the merger.

The Latham Tax Lawyer did not issue the opinion, ETE refused to close, and Williams sued, alleging that ETE breached the merger agreement by failing to use its best efforts to obtain the opinion. Williams asserted that ETE breached the merger agreement by failing to use "commercially reasonable efforts" to obtain the 721 opinion from Latham and "reasonable best efforts" to complete the transaction and, therefore, could not rely on the failure of the 721-opinion condition to terminate the agreement.

The Court of Chancery rejected Williams' arguments.

The Court of Chancery concluded that Latham's determination that it could not issue the 721 opinion was a good faith determination made by it independent of any conduct by ETE.[8] Williams argued on appeal that the Court of Chancery erred by interpreting "commercially reasonable efforts" and "reasonable best efforts" as imposing on ETE only a negative duty not to obstruct performance of the Agreement. Williams further argued that the Court of Chancery erred by placing upon it the burden of proving that ETE's breach of covenants materially contributed to the failure of the closing condition and that it should have shifted that burden to ETE.

The Delaware supreme court sided with Vice Chancellor findings that:

> Williams has not pointed to other facts which [ETE] withheld from or misrepresented to Latham *that have caused it to withhold* the 721 Opinion. There was simply nothing that indicates that [ETE] has manipulated the knowledge or ability of Latham to render the 721 Opinion, or failed to fully inform Latham, or do anything else, whether or not commercially reasonable, *to obstruct* Latham's issuance of the condition-precedent 721Opinion, or that had a material effect on Latham's decision.

Therefore, the Supreme Court found no basis to that [ETE] was in material breach of the commercially reasonable efforts requirement, and that the record was barren of any indication that the action or inaction of the Partnership (other than simply drawing Latham's attention to the problem) contributed materially to Latham's inability to issue the 721 Opinion.

At the time ETE entered into the agreement, it desired the consummation of the Merger Agreement and likely would have wanted to address any problem that could result in *either* party terminating the agreement. Therefore, ETE did not breach its representations and warranties.

Notes

1. *In Martin Marietta Materials, Inc. v. Vulcan Materials Co.*, No. 7102-CS (Del. Ch. May 4, 2012).
2. *Titan Investment Fund II, LP v. Freedom Mortgage Corp.*
3. Siga Technologies, Inc. v. PharmAthene 132 A.3d 1108 (Del. 2015).
4. Gillenardo v. Connor Broad. Del. Co., 2002 WL 991,110, at *1 (Del. Super. Apr. 30, 2002).
5. Williams Cos. v. Energy Transfer Equity, 159 A.3d 264 (Del. 2017).
6. *Akorn*, Inc. v. *Fresenius Kabi* AG, 198 A. 3d 724 - 2018 (*Del. 2018).*
7. Williams Cos. v. Energyfer Equity, 159 A.3d 264 (Del. 2017).
8. Section 721 provides that "[n]o gain or loss shall be recognized to a partnership or to any of its partners in the case of a contribution of property to the partnership in exchange for an interest in the partnership."

CHAPTER 3

Due Diligence

3.1 General

M&A lawyers assist and provide advice concerning the drafting, negotiation, and performance of contracts for the sale of portions of the business. M&A transactions are among the most complex and significant events in the life of a firm—the consequences of which reverberate both internally and externally. Diligence is comprehensive and does not touch just the financial aspects of the target but if done thoroughly will be able to provide you with a complete strategic assessment of the target from its operations to its management's capabilities. A diligence process that addresses priorities on a real-time basis and focuses on the most critical elements of the transaction: legal, financial, operational, and cultural is more than necessary to secure all the steps of the mergers and acquisitions.

3.2 Legal Due Diligence

Legal due diligence is the process of collecting, understanding, and assessing all the legal risks associated during a M&A process. The idea behind this investigation is to understand if there will be any future legal problems due to this acquisition Companies considering acquisitions must carefully review their target's contracts for anti-assignment clauses that prohibit assignment "by operation of law," which

F. Lessambo, *U.S. Mergers and Acquisitions*,
https://doi.org/10.1007/978-3-030-85735-6_3

Delaware courts interpret to include certain mergers. Due diligence seeks to understand all of a company's obligations, such as debts, pending and potential lawsuits, leases, warranties, long-term agreements, contracts, distribution agreements, compensation, and more.

In MTA Cathat, following a merger, the surviving company lacked standing to enforce a contract entered into by its predecessor (the non-surviving company in the merger) because the contract's anti-assignment clause prohibited assignment "by operation of law." The relevant facts under this case were the following:

- In 2016, Compania Minera Pangea, S.A. de C.V. ("CMP") purchased mineral rights in the El Gallo Mine from 1,570,926 Alberta Ltd. ("Alberta"). In exchange, CMP paid Alberta $5.25 m in cash at closing and agreed to pay Alberta an additional $1m in 2018 subject to certain conditions. Of note, the agreement contained the following anti-assignment clause (the "Anti-Assignment Clause"):

> Neither this Agreement nor any of the rights, interests or obligations under this Agreement may be assigned or delegated, in whole or in part, by operation of law or otherwise, by [Alberta] without the prior written consent of each other party, and any such assignment without such prior written consent shall be null and void. . . . [T]his Agreement will be binding upon, inure to the benefit of, and be enforceable by, the parties and their respective successors and assigns.

- In July 2017, Alberta merged with Global Royalty Corp. ("Global"), a subsidiary of Metalla Royalty & Streaming Ltd., and Global was the surviving entity. Following that transaction, Global changed its name to MTA Canada Royalty Corp. ("MTA").
- In November 2019, MTA brought a breach of contract claim against CMP based on CMP's alleged failure to pay the $1m in consideration due in 2018.
- CMP argued that MTA lacked standing to enforce Alberta's contract with CMP because, per the Anti-Assignment Clause, Alberta was required to obtain CMP's written consent before assigning its rights to MTA.

- MTA argued that the Anti-Assignment Clause was meant to prevent third-party assignments, not "successor assignments" like Alberta's merger.
- To make this argument, it relied on a 1993 Chancery decision, in which then-Vice Chancellor Jacobs had held that, subject to certain conditions, anti-assignment clauses do not apply to mergers unless mergers are explicitly prohibited.[1]
- According to MTA, because the last sentence of the Anti-Assignment Clause referred to "successors," it was clearly not intended to extend to mergers.
- The Superior Court disagreed. It explained that, because of the merger, Alberta had ceased to exist, so MTA could only enforce the contract if it showed that the Anti-Assignment Clause did not apply.
- It then held that the Anti-Assignment Clause clearly barred Alberta's transfer of rights through a merger because the clause prevented assignment "by operation of law," which Delaware case law had interpreted as referring to forward triangular mergers. In light of what is regarded as a straightforward application of the Anti-Assignment Clause.
- The Superior Court found that the reference to "successors" in the Anti-Assignment Clause meant only that "valid successors" had the right to enforce the contract.

3.3 Financial Due Diligence: Specialist Implications

Specialists involved in an M&A include investment bankers, management consultants, attorneys, accountants, as well as staff people from his company to analyze a prospective acquisition. Although specialization is a key part of decision-making in many organizational settings, the resulting isolation of specialists in acquisitions leads to a lack of integration in their analyses.

3.3.1 The Investment Bankers

Investment bankers are often referred to as "market makers," since they perform the functions of both a buyer and seller. Investment banks participate in mergers and acquisitions as either seller representation or buyer representation. One of the main roles of investment banks in mergers and acquisitions is to establish fair value for the companies involved in the transaction. They use financial models to capture the most important fixed and variable financial components that could influence the overall value of a company. Because of their expertise in business valuation, investment banks also provide the service of arbitrage opportunities for their clients. For instance, if a bank has performed valuation on a potential target company that suggests its market value (or the value of its shares in the marketplace) is less than what the business is actually worth, it may facilitate a merger or acquisition of this target company for its client that carries with it substantial profit opportunity. Investment banks also initiate deals by approaching businesses and suggesting M&A opportunities. They may suggest that two companies merge, or that one company acquires, or sells to, another. Investment banks contact the firms (clients) willing to purchase, to structure an acceptable offer.

3.3.2 *The Management Consultants*

Consulting companies are indispensable parts in any mergers and acquisitions. Management consultants develop tactics for the transaction, evaluate the target company, and speculate with stock prices of potential transaction candidates. The role of management consultants in the process of mergers and acquisitions is to advise in the whole process and negotiate within companies, provide assistance to the appropriate team of experts, co-ordinate the advice received from other professionals (i.e., lawyers), advice on financing the transaction. Mostly, management consultant services in mergers and acquisitions take place in several phases of the M&A process: (i) planning prior to the transaction, (ii) integration plan and implementation and in the end, and (iii) evaluation of transaction and activities after the transaction. In the first phase, the consultants must determine that the top management is fully aware of the activities that follow and those they are aligned with the strategic goals of the organization. The major activities of the preparations for the integration phase consist of appointment of personnel responsible for the integration process, development of communication plan, and establishment of a unified organizational structure of the merged company, making decisions about the necessary changes and assessing their effects, and making an integration plan. In the next phase, management consultants' efforts focus on the implementation of the transaction. That is, finding ways to achieve the best possible cooperation and communication between the two companies, organizing meetings of top management of both companies, and solving problems and disagreements that may arise. Lastly, in the post-integration phase, management consultants follow the process of mergers and acquisitions, calculate return period, adjust the organizational structure of the two organizations, address the issue of back-office technology, manage change and technology, and possibly correct unwanted behavior and reactions. To avoid organizational problems, the consultants in collaboration with management prepare employees for change.[2]

3.3.3 *The Accountants*

Accountants play an important role in mergers and acquisition transactions. The role varies in accordance with the M&A transaction at stake. They support the transaction teams in understanding the impact of identified accounting and tax issues and provide solutions to the identified issues such as modifications to the valuation assumptions, modifications to transaction structures, and others. Accountants are involved in all phases of mergers and acquisition, from the pre-acquisition review to the closing of the transaction. During the pre-acquisition phase, accountants gather information concerning the target (i.e., industry performance and forecast), recast financial statements and perform financial analysis; evaluate pricing models; determine initial structure and prepare for initial negotiations. In the planning and structuring phase, accountants assess buyer and seller tax issues (i.e., stock versus asset purchase, purchase of a subsidiary, tax-free reorganization, reverse triangular mergers, NOL limitations; structure leveraged recap, pooling vs. purchase, etc.). Depending on the skills, most accountants are involved in structuring the deal and other tax due diligence.

3.4 Organizational Due Diligence

Organizational Due diligence (aka Management due diligence) aims to assess and understand the extent to which the seller will fit strategically within the larger buyer organization. A sound organizational due diligence provides understanding the culture of the organizations involved in a M&A, as well as the roles, capabilities, and attitudes of the people from or within the two organizations.[3] Through organizational due diligence, the buyer reviews a number of matters in order to understand the quality of the seller's management and employee base. AQ carefully conducted organization due diligence provides the following benefits:

- It ensures sustainable profit and growth for organizations, as it identifies the human capital components. It does so by ensuring that highly skilled people are assigned the correct jobs and responsibilities.
- It identifies strengths and weaknesses of individuals in the management team and assesses their contributions to the organization.
- It assesses management team members' abilities to reach common goals.
- It helps organizations efficiently appraise candidates for a management team position.
- Gives an organization a basis for expectations for team and individual performance. Accordingly, the organization can determine whether managers need training.

It should be noticed that managerial due diligence is often challenging in hostile takeover situations. Nonetheless, there is still a certain amount of human due diligence that companies can and must do to reduce the inevitable fallout from the acquisition process and smooth the integration.[4]

Example

The Chinese company Lenovo's acquisition of IBM's PC business, completed in May 2005, is a case in point. In fact, the board of Lenovo's controlling shareholder allowed the company to pursue the deal if, and only if, it could recruit IBM's senior executives to manage the merged enterprise. Lenovo's interest was not just in the top people. The company offered a job to every IBM employee with no obligation to relocate or accept reduced compensation. That meant the company could continue seamlessly on its way, with minimal disruption of engineering projects or customer relationships.

Both Lenovo and IBM PC Division worked harder to create a common organizational culture:

> *We had tried our best to stabilize the emotion of employees… and we wanted to get a common culture… the two companies had the similar value and vision, such as integrity and responsibility… so, we created a unified culture background to strengthen cultural identity gradually.* (Zhou and Haung 2014: 38)

The Chinese had spent the period of upheaval learning about the capabilities needed within a multinational company. They came to the United States ready to learn and absorb expertise.

Not every company, of course, wants to retain all its target's managers, and most will need to determine who goes and who stays. Working that out requires the same kind of detailed assessment that goes into any high-level hiring effort. Acquisition team members should gather performance reviews, interview third parties (recruiters and former executives, for instance), and assess the executives' records of accomplishment. They should probe the executives' leadership styles and evaluate how they have dealt with difficult decisions. Most of all, acquisition team members should simply spend time with their counterparts in the target company, preferably on the target's turf, getting to know them as individuals.

The investment bankers who entertain an acquisition team at the target company's facilities will always want team members to spend their time in conference rooms, focusing on the performance story and numbers. Nevertheless, every visit to a target is also a chance to get out and learn firsthand how the organization feels.

Notes

1. *Star Cellular Tel. Co. v. Baton Rouge CGSA.*, 1993 Del. Ch. LEXIS 158, at *25 (July 30, 1993).
2. Filipovic, Davor; Kandzija, Tomislav & Pavlovic, Ana: Overview on Consultants' Activity in M&A Processes, Annals of DAAAM for 2012 & Proceedings of the 23rd International DAAAM Symposium, Volume 23, No. 1, ISSN 2304–1382.
3. David Harding and Ted Rouse (2007) Human Due Diligence, Harvard Business Review.
4. David Harding and Ted Rouse (2007) Human Due Diligence, Harvard Business Review.

CHAPTER 4

Mergers and Acquisitions Financing

4.1 General

Mergers and acquisitions can be financed in various ways. Primary forms of *M&A Financing* include debt or equity, or the hybrid of the two. Within each of these primary forms, there are a variety of different structures differentiated by term, pricing, position, and risk tolerance. The purpose of M&A financing is to fund an acquisition for a purchaser and to provide the capital within a structure that is sensitive to the operating cash flow reality of the company. M&A Financing can be in the form of publicly traded securities such as stocks, bonds, and convertible securities. It most frequently takes the form of a bank loan, a mezzanine loan, and private equity for middle-market companies.

4.2 Types of M&A Financing

4.2.1 Company Funds

It is possible to acquire business by means of a transaction, which is 100% cash financed. However, although the vast majority of acquisitions involve some upfront cash payment, it is remarkably rare to finance the entire deal in this manner. Company funds or cash purchasing is the most obvious alternative to paying for a transaction with stock. While cash payment is the preferred method, the price of M&A transactions can run into the millions or even billions, and not many companies can access this much

F. Lessambo, *U.S. Mergers and Acquisitions*,
https://doi.org/10.1007/978-3-030-85735-6_4

cash from their own funds. In cash transactions, acquiring shareholders take on the entire risk that the expected synergy value embedded in the acquisition premium will not materialize.[1]

But there are ways of obtaining cash from others ahead of an upcoming M&A transaction:

- IPO

An initial public offering (IPO) refers to the process of offering shares of a private corporation to the public in a new stock issuance. Public share issuance allows a company to raise **capital** from public investors. The prospect of an upcoming M&A transaction can make investors more excited about the company's future, as it signals an ambition to expand and a long-term strategy. Moreover, increasing the value of an IPO with an upcoming M&A transaction increases the value of existing shares—in fact, existing shareholders could see their stock value rocket overnight. In 2020, the world has seen the highest IPO capital raising activity in a decade, with USD 331 billion raised across 1591 listings—a 42% increase compared to 2019.[2]

- Bond issuance

Issuing bonds is an excellent way to fund the acquisition of a business. Corporate bonds are a quick and easy way of getting cash, either from existing shareholders or from members of the public. In purchasing these bonds, investors are essentially loaning money to the company in the expectation that they will receive a return on their capital over time, but once the investment has been made, their money is locked in and cannot be touched until the lifetime of the bonds. It is worthy to mention that the length of the M&A process can take anywhere from six months to several years, depending on the complexity of the deal. Thus, managing potential interest rate exposure inevitably becomes a top priority for issuers. Interest rate forecast and sensitivity analysis can help issuers optimize bond issuance strategy with respect to timing, term, and hedging. Likewise, establishing an understanding of historical credit spread volatility is critical to the success of bond issuance. Finally, most M&A-driven bond issues include some type of special mandatory redemption clauses, also known as escrow features that require the issuer to redeem all outstanding bonds at a predetermined redemption price provided the acquisition be not consummated prior to a predetermined redemption date.

- Loans

Borrowing money can be an expensive affair when undertaking an M&A transaction. Lenders, or owners who have agreed to accept payments over an extended period, will demand a reasonable interest rate for the loans they have made. Even when the interest is relatively small, when you are dealing with a multi-million-dollar M&A transaction, the costs can really add up. Interest rates, therefore, are an important consideration in funding M&A transactions with debt, and low-interest rates will spike the number of transactions funded with loans. In 2015, for instance, loans became very popular following central banks' quantitative easing programs, which greatly reduced US interest rates. In the first two quarters of 2015, the amount of debt ($290 billion) used to fund mergers and acquisitions was triple the amount used in that period of 2014.

4.2.2 Company Equity (or Exchanging Stock)

Offering equity to the owners of a target firm can be an excellent way of smoothing the process, particularly where they are interested in maintaining some control. This is probably the most common option when it comes to financing an M&A deal. In a typical stock-exchange transaction, the acquirer exchanges its shares for shares in the acquiree firm. Financing M&A with stock is advantageous to a buyer if its shares are overvalued on the market, as the acquirer will receive more stocks in the seller company per shares exchanged than if they were paying for their transaction in cash. In a merger deal, shareholders on both sides can reap the benefits of a stock-swap in the long term, as they will generally receive an equal amount of stock in the newly formed company that results from the transaction, rather than simply receiving money for their shares. However, there is one major drawback to using stock as currency to pay for M&A—stock volatility. No matter how well a company is doing, there is always a risk of a drop in stock, particularly if word gets out about a possible M&A before any deal has been finalized. Stock markets thrive on liquidity, so shareholders can move quickly to sell their stock if they have any reason to feel nervous about the future of a particular company. An unannounced or unexplained M&A deal would certainly raise a few questions in the financial press. Furthermore, global financial events can wreak havoc on share prices, no matter how well the company is doing. Most famously, the global financial crisis knocked trillions of dollars off the value of global stock markets, and the recent Brexit fallout saw the popular London Stock Exchange hit dangerous lows. Stocks are also subject to artificial market movements, such as shorting, although there are regulatory instruments in place to prevent this from having a seriously adverse effect on a company's value.

While it is hard to predict what shares will be worth in the future, it is easy to understand why some companies might be reluctant to sell their shares in exchange for stock rather than cash. Often a compromise is reached whereby the sale price includes a mix of shares and cash, reducing risk on both sides and allowing both parties to maintain a stake in the new company.

4.2.3 Mezzanine or Quasi Debt

Mezzanine or quasi-debt is an integrated form of financing that includes both equity and debt features. It usually comes with an option of being converted to equity. A mezzanine fund is a pool of capital, which invests in mezzanine finance for acquisitions, growth, recapitalization, or management/leveraged buyouts. In the capital structure of a company, mezzanine finance is a hybrid between equity and debt. Mezzanine financing most commonly takes the form of preferred stock or subordinated and unsecured debts. Mezzanine financing is suitable for target companies with a strong balance sheet and steady profitability. Mezzanine lenders assess creditworthiness through stability of the company's cash flow over time. The loan is viewed as a multiple of the businesses earnings before interest, taxes, depreciation, and amortization (EBITDA). Market multiples usually range from 2.5 to 4.0 times EBITDA. A mezzanine lender charges an interest rate and participates in the upside of the company through a warrant. Such an approach is often praised as it aligns the mutual objective of the lender and the company to pursue growth. Finally, mezzanine lenders are often long-termists.

4.2.4 Earn-out

An earn-out is one of the most creative ways to finance an acquisition. In general, earn-out agreements stipulate that acquirers withhold a portion of the total merger consideration until target managers achieve pre-specified performance objectives. These objectives are typically related to post-merger performance measures such as cash flows, sales, or earnings.[3] Under the earn-out financing, the seller receives a portion of the sale price upfront, with the opportunity to earn the rest of the agreed-upon sale price based on the company's continued performance.

An earn-out is a practical financial tool for an instance when a gap exists between the valuation price and allotted funding from the buyer. Earn-out agreements can also provide an important liquidity management tool to financially constrained acquirers.However, earn-out rewards can be difficult to measure when the deal involves merging two existing businesses. In addition, earn-outs can provide financial slack to managers when other sources of funds are unavailable or prohibitively costly. Such a financial constraint can lead firms to seek credit arrangements with non-financial institutions.[5] The earn-out value derives from a variety of achievement determiners, depending on whatever measures the parties agreed upon. Future revenues calculate the most common variable for earn-out value determiners. An earn-out can be paid in either installments or a lump sum at the end of the determined period.

4.2.5 Leveraged Buyout

A leveraged buyout (LBO) is a type of M&A financing which allows companies to make large acquisitions without having to commit significant amounts of their own capital or money. Rather, the assets of the company being purchased are used for collateral of the loans as well as the assets of the company itself. LBO allows companies to make large acquisitions without having to make the commitment of a lot of capital. The ratio is usually 70% debt to 90% with 10–30% of it being equity. Capital for an LBO can come from banks, mezzanine financing, and bond issues. In general, the acquirer will consider such financing in situations where he considers the target firm is undervalued or underperforming, with potential for improving operationally and financially under new ownership and control. Thus, the acquirer sees that there is an opportunity of making a good return on the investment. LBO can be traced back as far as the late 1960s.[6]

The first leveraged buyout may have been the purchase by McLean Industries, Inc. of Pan-Atlantic Steamship Company in January 1955 and Waterman Steamship Corporation in May 1955. Under the terms of that transaction, McLean borrowed $42 million and raised an additional $7 million through an issue of preferred stock. On January 21, 1955, McLean Industries, Inc. purchased the capital stock of Pan-Atlantic Steamship Corporation and Gulf Florida Terminal Company, Inc. from Waterman Steamship Corporation. In May McLean Industries, Inc. completed the acquisition of the common stock of Waterman Steamship Corporation from its founders and other stockholders.

The buyout process typically commences when an interested acquirer formally makes a buyout offer to the board of directors. Private individuals, companies, private equity firms, supply the funds used in buyout transactions. The funds can also come from the management of the target. A management buyout occurs when the existing management team of a company acquires all or a significant part of the company from the private owners or the parent company. In a typical LBO, a smaller number of shareholders following the acquisition owns the target's equity.[7] Likewise, in most LBO, new management often takes advantage of the debt capacity of the target's assets, hence looks for low debt in the target firm. Nonetheless, LBOs carry a higher level of risk than other financial transactions considering the significant amounts of debt involved. LBOs affect the debt structure of the acquirer and lead to an increase in loan payments on the company's books. If the combined companies cannot meet their debt obligations using the combined cash flow of the two companies, the company being acquired may go bankrupt. In some cases, both the acquiring company and the company being purchased can go bankrupt.

The LBO pricing model is employed by financial sponsors to determine whether and how much to bid when proposing a leveraged buyout, like an MBO, and "solves for the range of prices that a financial sponsor can pay while still" achieving its target internal rate of return (IRR). According to the court, the range of prices resulting from an LBO model can differ significantly from fair value because of both the financial sponsor's need to achieve significant IRRs and "limits on the amount of leverage that the company can support and the sponsor can use to finance the deal." In re Appraisal of Dell Inc, the Court held:

> A claim that the bargained-for price in an MBO represents fair value should be evaluated with greater thoroughness and care than, at the other end of the spectrum, a transaction with a strategic buyer in which management will not be retained.

That is because management owns a substantial part of the firm, the separation between ownership and control has been reduced. For instance, in re Appraisal of Dell Inc, the Court found that the heavy influence of the LBO pricing model on the bidding process distorted the process. Managers may become excessively focused on these performance measures rather than on the long-term interests of the firm. Moreover, financial measures may be subject to manipulation by the managers themselves.

- In re Appraisal of Dell Inc.

> *Dell* establishes that MBOs present special issues in the appraisal context and warrant careful consideration by the court when deciding whether the deal price should influence its determination of fair value. The facts of the case can be summarized as follow:

- Michael Dell proposed a management buyout (MBO) of Dell, Inc. (the company).
- The buyout was a step in the process of transforming the company from an end-user hardware supplier to an enterprise customer software and services supplier.
- Dell Inc. financial sponsor during the merger process used a leveraged buyout (LBO) pricing model to evaluate offers.
- Dell Inc. board of directors reached a deal with a buyout group for $13.65 per share.
- After shareholders objected, the buyout group offered $13.75 per share, and 57 percent of Dell Inc. shares voted in favor of the merger.
- The merger agreement permitted a go-shop period, but Dell Inc. did not receive any better offers.
- Shareholders who dissented from the merger filed a petition seeking judicial appraisal of their shares.
- Dell Inc. argued that the merger consideration was the best evidence of fair value.

- The Chancery Court found that several aspects of both the pre- and post-signing phases undercut the reliability of the deal price as an indicator of fair value: (1) the heavy influence of the LBO pricing model on the bidding process; (2) lack of meaningful competition among prospective bidders; and (3) evidence of a significant gap between the company's intrinsic value and the market's perception of the company's value.
- Moreover, the court found that because the merger consideration resulting from the pre-signing phase of the process was dictated by what a financial sponsor could pay and still generate outsized returns, it necessarily "undervalued the company as a going concern."

Another interesting case that illustrates LBO hurdles is the Smith case:

- Smith v. Van Gorkom, 488 A.2d 858 (Del. 1985).

- Trans Union had large investment tax credits (ITCs) coupled with accelerated depreciation deductions with no offsetting taxable income.
- The Chief Financial Officer, Donald Romans, suggested that Trans Union undergo a leveraged buyout to an entity that could offset the ITCs.
- The suggestion came without any substantial research, but Romans thought that a \$50–60 share price (on stock currently valued at a high of \$39½) would be acceptable.
- Van Gorkom did not demonstrate any interest in the suggestion, but shortly thereafter pursued the idea with a takeover specialist, Jay Pritzker.
- Van Gorkom sets up an agreement with Pritzker to sell Pritzker Trans Union shares at \$55 per share. Van Gorkom also agreed to sell Pritzker one million shares of Trans Union at \$39 per share if Pritzker was outbid.
- Van Gorkom also agreed not to solicit other bids and agreed not to provide proprietary information to other bidders.
- Van Gorkom only included a couple people in the negotiations with Pritzker, and most of the senior management and the Board of Directors found out about the deal on the day they had to vote to approve the deal.

- Van Gorkom did not distribute any information at the voting, so the Board had only the word of Van Gorkom, the word of the President of Trans Union (who was privy to the earlier discussions with Pritzker), advice from an attorney who suggested that the Board might be sued if they voted against the merger, and vague advice from Romans who told them that the $55 was in the beginning end of the range he calculated.
- Van Gorkom did not disclose how he came to the $55 amount. On this advice, the Board approved the merger, and it was also later approved by shareholders.

4.2.6 Asset-Backed Loan

An asset-backed loan is similar to a leveraged buyout in that you are essentially using the value generated by the target company to acquire it. Asset-backed financing is a method of debt financing where banks can lend funds based on the collateral offered by the target company. The size of your asset-based loan is calculated on a percentage of the combined value of your accounts receivable, inventory, equipment, and in special circumstances, real estate. This allows a firm to turn its assets into working capital and access flexible funding quickly. In general, an asset-backed loan is made on the basis that the assets of the target firm can be liquidated in the worst-case scenario.

4.2.7 Joint Venture

Although technically not a method of financing, entering an acquisition through a joint venture (JV) with another firm can be an excellent way to gain (joint) control of a business, with a lower upfront cost.

There are several caveats, however. It can be challenging to find a suitable JV partner, as many joint ventures destroy value as creating it, and your efforts to make management decisions at the acquired business may be stifled in the end by virtue of controlling less of its equity. Nevertheless, where two businesses can find the right harmony, the combined expertise provided by two sets of management can generate considerably more value.

Legal Insight
The RJR Nabisco Case

RJR Nabisco's buyout is the largest, most controversial, hostile, and aggressive takeover in the history of the private equity industry.

- Reynolds Tobacco Holdings, Inc. ("RJR"), the parent company of R.J. Reynolds Tobacco Company, a leading manufacturer of cigarette and tobacco products, completed its acquisition of the U.S. business of Brown & Williamson Tobacco Corporation ("B&W"), a U.S. subsidiary of British American Tobacco p.l.c. ("BAT").
- The transaction combined the second- and third-largest U.S. cigarette and tobacco businesses.
- In addition, RJR acquired Lane Limited, a former BAT subsidiary that manufactures various tobacco brands and distributes Dunhill cigarettes.
- As part of the transaction, a new publicly traded company, Reynolds American Inc. (RAI), was formed, with an equity value of approximately $10 billion.
- Because of the transaction, former RJR public stockholders own 58 percent of RAI, and BAT owns the remaining 42 percent. Based on 2002 results, RAI would have annual revenues of approximately $10 billion and account for more than 30 percent of U.S. cigarette sales. The parties expect synergies from the transaction to generate at least $500 million in annual cost savings.
- The enterprise value of the deal was then estimated at $31 billion, which today is equivalent to approximately $65 billion.
- KKR introduced a tender offer to obtain RJR Nabisco for $90 per share—a price that enabled it to proceed without the approval of RJR Nabisco's management.
- KKR assumed that tobacco *sales and operating income* would grow by 8.3 per cent and by more than 10 percent per year, respectively.
- RJR's management team, working with Shearson Lehman Hutton and Salomon Brothers, submitted a bid of $112, a figure they felt certain would enable it to outflank any response by Kravis.
- KKR's final bid of $109, while a lower dollar figure, was ultimately accepted by the board of directors. It was accepted because KKR's offer was guaranteed, whereas management's lacked a "reset", meaning that the final share price might have been lower than their professed $112 per share.

- Additionally, many in RJR's board of directors had grown concerned at recent disclosures of Johnson's unprecedented severance agreement deal.

Notes

1. Alfred Rappaport and Mark L. Sirower (2016): Stock or Cash?: The Trade-Offs for Buyers and Sellers in Mergers and Acquisitions, Harvard Business Review.
2. Baker McKenzie's IPO Report 2020.
3. Thomas Bates, Jordan B. Neyland, Yolanda Yulong Wang (2017): Financing Acquisitions with Earn-outs.
4. Thomas Bates, Jordan B. Neyland, Yolanda Yulong Wang (2017): Financing Acquisitions with Earn-outs, p. 2.
5. Thomas Bates, Jordan B. Neyland, Yolanda Yulong Wang (2017): Financing Acquisitions with Earn-outs, p. 8.
6. The acquisitions were called "bootstrap" transactions.
7. Christina M. Sauter (2020): Delaware as Deal Arbiter, Washington and Lee Law Review, Volume 77 Issue 3 Article 7, p. 1279.

CHAPTER 5

The Fiduciary Duties

5.1 General

Directors of a Delaware corporation owe two fiduciary duties—care and loyalty. The duty of loyalty includes a requirement to act in good faith, which is a subsidiary element. Directors must exercise their independent fiduciary judgment: Delaware law confers the management of the corporate enterprise to the stockholders duly elected board representatives. The fiduciary duty to manage a corporate enterprise includes the selection of a time- frame for achievement of corporate goals. That duty may not be delegated to the stockholders. The "duty of disclosure is not an independent duty, but derives from the duties of care and loyalty." The duty of disclosure arises because of "the application in a specific context of the board's fiduciary duties …." Its scope and requirements depend on context; the duty "does not exist in a vacuum."

Courts in the US, and particularly the Delaware Chancery and Supreme Courts have developed specific standards to ascertain the board actions. The directors of Delaware corporations have a triad of primary fiduciary duties: (i) due care; (ii) loyalty; and (iii) good faith. However, the Delaware courts adhere to the view that management owes fiduciary duty of care and loyalty to the corporation and its stakeholders. Simultaneously,[1] such an approach has been characterized by Professor

F. Lessambo, *U.S. Mergers and Acquisitions*,
https://doi.org/10.1007/978-3-030-85735-6_5

Christopher Bruner as a "decided reluctance to focus solely on the shareholders, to the exclusion of the other constituencies contributing to the corporate enterprise."[2]

- Duty of Care

Directors must discharge their duty in good faith, with such a degree of diligence, care, and skill than an ordinary prudent person would exercise under similar circumstances. Directors would be held responsible for either non-feasance or misfeasance, any time their inaction or action causes harm to the corporation.

The duty of care requires directors to take certain responsibilities or actions. In Francis v. United Jersey Bank,[3] the New Jersey Supreme Court held that:

Directors should have some understanding of the business, keep informed on activities, perform general monitoring including attendance at meetings, and have some familiarity with the financial status of the business as reflected on the financial statements.

However, the company certificate of incorporation may shield the directors from the liability pursuant to their duty of care if the breach and the harm suffered by the corporation did not occur in bad faith or with an intentional misconduct of disregard.

To establish that a director has failed to act in good faith, a shareholder must show whether that the director conduct was motivated by an actual intent to do harm or that the director acted with a conscientious disregard as to his (her) fiduciary duties.

In In Re Walt Disney Co. Derivative Litigation, the Delaware Court has held:

Fiduciary action taken solely due to gross negligence and without any malevolent intent does not constitute bad faith.[4]

- Duty of Loyalty

The duty of loyalty mandates that the best interest of the corporation and its shareholders take precedence over any interest possessed by a director, officer, or controlling shareholder and not shared by the stockholders generally. A failure to act in good faith may be shown, for instance, where the fiduciary intentionally acts with a purpose other than that of advancing the best interests of the corporation.

Directors should perform their duty with loyalty. That is, directors must act (i) in good faith, (ii) with the conscientiousness, fairness, morality, and honesty that the law requires of fiduciaries. The duty of loyalty prevents them for engaging in self-dealing, usurping the corporation opportunity, or making secret profits at the detriment of the corporation.

The duty of loyalty is often breached when directors engage in interested transactions. Such transactions are suspicious and set aside, unless the directors establish that the transactions were fair and reasonable at the time their entered into; or have disclosed the material facts and won the approval of the Board.

Likewise, directors should not usurp the corporation's business opportunity. This refers to any business or transaction the corporation has a tangible interest or expectancy in, or logically related to the corporation core and auxiliary businesses.

- Good Faith Conduct

The Delaware courts are still struggling to provide clear opinions concerning Delaware directors' duty to act in good faith. The duty to act in good faith has been described simultaneously as a third component of the triad of primary fiduciary duties, or confusingly as an aspect of the duty of care or the duty of loyalty.

In the Walt Disney cases,[5] the duty to act in good faith was described as an independent duty from the two other duties (care and loyalty).

The Delaware Supreme Court has stated that bad faith conduct may be found where a director "intentionally acts with a purpose other than that of advancing the best interests of the corporation, ... acts with the intent to violate applicable positive law, or ... intentionally fails to act in the face of a known duty to act, demonstrating a conscious disregard for his duties."

However, in subsequent cases, the Delaware court hold that directors would be liable for bad faith if the facts establish an intentional dereliction of duty, a conscious disregard as to their responsibilities.[6]

- Duty of Disclosure

There is no independent duty of disclosure under Delaware law. Instead, the duty of disclosure derives from the duty of care and the duty of loyalty.

In Malone v. Brincat,[7] the Delaware Supreme Court explained that directors owe a duty not to speak falsely:

Whenever directors communicate publicly or directly with shareholders about the corporation's affairs, with or without a request for shareholder action, directors have a fiduciary duty to shareholders to exercise due care, good faith, and loyalty. It follows a fortiori that when directors communicate publicly or directly with shareholders about corporate matters, the sine qua non of directors' fiduciary duty to shareholders is honesty.

5.2 Fiduciary Duties to a Third Party

Under settled Delaware law, however, the directors and officers owe fiduciary duties to the corporation and its stockholders. In other words, a corporation does not owe fiduciary duties to its stockholders. However, a third party may be liable for aiding and abetting a breach of a corporate fiduciary's duty to the stockholders if the third party knowingly participates' in the breach. The complaint must satisfy four elements: (1) the existence of a fiduciary relationship; (2) a breach of the fiduciary duty; (3) knowing participation in that breach by the defendants; and (4) damages.

Put differently, proving liability under an aiding and abetting theory comes down to what constitutes knowing participation. The element of the aiding and abetting test requires an understanding between the parties with respect to their complicity in any scheme to defraud or in any breach of fiduciary duties. That is, the third party aider-and-abettor possessed the requisite degree of scienter or knowing participation.

In Del Monte, the Court held that an acquirer is free to seek the lowest possible price through arms' length negotiations.

5.3 Fiduciary Duties in Short-Form Merger

In a short-form merger, however, the Section 253—authorizes a summary procedure that is inconsistent with any reasonable notion of fair dealing. Controlling stockholders continue to owe fiduciary duties, and although Section 253 displaces both the fair process and fair price aspects of the entire fairness inquiry, it does not eliminate the need for disclosure.

By authorizing a parent corporation to eliminate minority stockholders through the simple expedient of filing a certificate of ownership and merger, the General Assembly cabined the role of equity and eliminated the aspect of fair process.

5.4 The Safeguards: The Business Judgment Rules

The "Business Judgment Rule" principle can be traced back in the US to the "Harvard College and Massachusetts General Hospital v. Francis Amory" case in 1830, where judge Samuel Putnam asserted: "trustee cannot be held accountable for bad outcomes except for gross neglect and willful mismanagement. In the same vein, the Supreme court of Michigan went on to add in Dodge v. Ford" that the best judgment rule must include long-term consideration.

5.4.1 The BJT: A Review Standard

Delaware's default standard of review is the business judgment rule, a principle of non-review that reflects and promotes the role of the board of directors as the proper body to manage the business and affairs of the corporation. The rule presumes that—in making a business decision, the directors of a corporation acted on an informed basis, in good faith, and in the honest belief that the action taken was in the best interests of the company. Unless one of its elements is rebutted—the court merely looks to see whether the business decision made was rational in the sense of being one logical approach to advancing the corporation's objectives. Only when a decision lacks any rationally conceivable basis will a court infer bad faith and a breach of duty.

The business judgment rule (BJR) protects the board of directors against suits that derive from a violation of the duty of care or malfeasance. It protects directors who are not negligent while making decisions for the corporation. Generally, Courts will not second-guess the board decision even when it is damageable to the business. The rule introduces a rebuttable presumption that in making a business decision, the directors of a corporation acted on an informed basis, in good faith, and in the honest belief that the action taken was in the best interests of the company. The directors must show that they had reasonable grounds for believing that a danger to corporate policy and effectiveness existed.

Further, they must show that the defensive mechanism was "reasonable in relation to the threat posed."

Moreover, that proof is materially enhanced, as in UNOCAL,[8] where a majority of the board favoring the proposal consisted of outside independent directors who have acted in accordance with the foregoing standards. The safeguard of the best judgment rule shields directors even if "hindsight later reveals other choices that arguably were better or wiser." The shareholders can overcome the presumption by establishing malfeasance or breach of duty of care. When the directors were grossly negligent as in the Van Gorkom case,[9] the Chancery Court has no difficulty finding a breach of duty of care.

In applying the best judgment rule, the Delaware courts have elaborated specific requirements that the boards must meet. These requirements or standards are often referred to as either the Revlon standard,[10] or the Unocal standard,[11] or the Paramount standard.[12] The board must demonstrate that: (i) it had reasonable grounds for believing that a danger to corporate policy and effectiveness existed,[13] and (ii) its defensive actions were reasonable in relation to the threat posed.[14]

The Revlon court summarized both steps in the review as follows: (i) when a board implements anti-takeover measures, there arises a rebuttable presumption that a board may be acting primarily in its own interests, rather than those of the corporation and its shareholders; (ii) the directors must analyze the nature of the takeover and its effect on the corporation in order to ensure balance.

The Court also held that when the sale of the target becomes inevitable, the board must have then been working on getting the maximum price of the company for the benefit of the shareholders. Applying this principle to the facts, the court come to find that the board entered into an auction-ending lock-up agreement with Fortsman on the basis of impermissible considerations at the expense of the shareholders.

In both Revlon and Paramount, the Court held that lock-up clauses are invalid when it favored a Bidder, but did allow termination fees. Defendants in the Paramount case contended that they were precluded from negotiating with QVC or seeking alternative. After considering the merit of the facts, the court held:

Such provision, whether or not they are presumptively valid in the abstract, may not validly define or limit the directors; fiduciary duties under Delaware law or prevent the Paramount directors from carrying out their fiduciary duties under the Delaware law.

In the Unocal case, the Delaware Supreme Court sets forth a list of elements or factors to consider in assessing the existence of the threat to the target corporation. These factors include, inter alia: the inadequacy of the offered price, the nature and timing of the offer, the impact on constituencies other than shareholders, the risk of non-consumption, the quality of securities being offered in the exchange process. However, none of in these factors alone should be, per se, considered controlling in the examination process.

In Phelps Dodge Corp,[15] the court held that a merger agreement that has a "no talk provision" is per se invalid. Phelps Dodge challenged Cyprus Amax merger agreement with Asarco, Inc., which included a "no talk" provision. After examining the merits of the case, the Delaware Chancery Court found that Cyprus Amax and Asarco should not have completely foreclosed the opportunity to negotiate. That their eager blindness constituted a breach of a board's duty of care.

In IXC Communications, the court held that directors need flexibility to lock-up deal. The Chancery Court was called to rule over the validity of a "no talk" provision that prevented the parties from entertaining other potential deals.

The Court rejected the plaintiffs claim that the board "eagerly blinded" itself by approving the "no talk" provision. The Chancery Court did so because the challenge "no talk" provision emerged later in the process, and that the parties had retracted the provision, permitting the board to hear any proposals it saw fit.

In Mills V. MacMillan,[16] the court invalidated a lock-up clause when it found the auction to be unfair.

In Omnicare v. NCS,[17] the court found the lock-up provisions to be preclusive and coercive. The lock-up by Genesis took the form of (i) voting agreement with majority shareholders, (ii) no-shop clause, (iii) termination fee of $6 million, and (iv) shareholder approval of the agreement. The court found that Omnicare enhanced its bid to shareholders only when it discovered that a competitor was buying NCS. More importantly, the Court found that the voting agreement and the vote requirement used as lock-up were preclusive and coercive.

While one can follow through the development of the aforementioned cases, the shield of the best judgment rule, except in a few cases, immunized sufficiently the board, and to certain extent the corporate officers from "strict" personal liability that proceed from their actions.[18]

Some have argued that directors and officers of publicly traded corporations should be held personally liable for their failure to live up to their fiduciary duties.

5.4.2 *Reforming the Best Judgment Rule*

The best judgment rule as developed by the Delaware Courts has become, to many respects, obsolete, or at least irrelevant. The Delaware Courts have to evolve toward an enhanced standard for direct with special skills, expertise, or knowledge as under the Federal tort laws. At some point, the Delaware Courts seemed to take such direction. In In Re Emerging Communications Shareholders Litigation,[19] the Court subjected the director with special expertise to an enhanced standard of the fiduciary duties (duty of care). Several applications by the Delaware Courts of the duty of care are inconsistent or at least shows that corporate judge needs to enhance their own skills while deciding some difficult case. In 2005, for instance, the Delaware Chancery Court stated in a shareholder lawsuit filed against the Walt Disney board, that although the action of the directors fell significantly short of the best practices of ideal corporate governance, the law "cannot hold fiduciaries liable for a failure to comply with the aspirational ideal of best practices."

The facts of the case could be summarized as follows:

- Michael Eisner, the chairperson of the Walt Disney authorized singularly a severance pay of $140 million for his friend Michael Ovitz who spent a little time as Walt Disney director.
- Walt Disney shareholders brought a legal action against the board alleging inter alia (i) harm to their investment and long-term commitment to Disney, and (ii) insufficient information concerning the severance package prior to the payment.

Despite all evidence, the Chancery Court ruled that the hastily approval and initial concealment of the agreement did not rise to the standard of action that intentionally creates or allows harm.

Recently, in In Re Citigroup, Inc.,[20] whereby the shareholders argued breach of fiduciary duty by the board of Citigroup, Inc., which failed to oversight the corporation risk management guidelines, the same court recanted from its position to hold that directors with special skills will be held to the same standard of conduct as any other.

The Court justified the board attitude under the best judgment rule, through a fallacious reasoning:

Citigroup was in the business of taking on and managing investment and other business risks. To impose oversight liability on directors for failure to monitor "excessive" risk would involve courts in conducting hindsight evaluations of decisions at the heart of the business judgment of directors. Oversight duties under Delaware law are not designed to subject director's even expert directors, to personal liability for failure to predict the future and to properly evaluate business risk.

While intellectually enticing for lecture within law schools, the Chancery Court ruling failed to consider the financial aspects of the banking, specifically the risk management side which the board should oversight to assess the officers' compliance therewith.

The facts from the record indicated that while facing liquidity shortage, the bank responded by creating collateral debt obligation (CDO), and the board seemed unaware of. Indeed, the OECD Corporate Governance Principle VI. D.2 makes it clear that, inter alia, the board consists of monitoring the effectiveness of a company's management practices and making changes as needed.

That anytime a board approves a company's strategy but failed to establish suitable metrics to monitor its implementation, its responsibility should be engaged. Furthermore, Principles 2 and 3 of the Basel Committee state, respectively:

The board of directors should approve and oversee the bank's strategic objectives and corporate values that are communicated through the banking organization.

The Board of directors should set and enforce clear lines of responsibility and accountability throughout the organization.

Obviously, the Board in "In Citigroup" case has failed to live up to its fiduciary duties that stemmed from both the Delaware General Corporate Laws and the international commitment from the OECD and the Basel Committee.

5.5 Corporate Defensive Tactics

Two defensive tactics have appeared to be more successful to US boards fighting back against hostile takeover: (a) the poison pill and (b) the staggered board.

5.5.1 Poison Pills

Prior to 1985, private equity firms and other corporate raiders threatened corporate boards with hostile takeover. Many corporate boards seemed powerless and could not resist the takeover tornadoes. Things dramatically changed in 1985, when the Delaware Chancery Court ruled for the validity of poison pill[21] as a defensive tactic. Initially, poison pills were aimed at protecting shareholders against a change of control that fails to provide shareholders with an appropriate control premium.

In Moran v. Household International Inc.,[22] the Delaware court, for the very first time, upheld the Household plan as a legitimate exercise of the board's business judgment. Whenever a bidder acquires more than the preset share of the target company's stock, poison pill will be triggered and allows all the shareholders of the target company, except the hostile bidder, to exercise their right to purchase additional stock at 50% discount. The final aim of a poison pill is to massively dilute the target equity, thus rendering the bid whether expensive or difficult.

Poison pills quickly transformed the landscape of defensive tactics available to corporate boards. However, the use of the device by the corporate boards triggered vehement criticisms on behalf of the takeovers. Some have argued that the mere existence of a poison pill violates the essence of corporate governance as it allows the board and not the shareholders to have a final say on the bid. Others have argued that the pill advances shareholders' interests by enabling a board to resist incentive takeover tactics and allows the corporate board to negotiate in good shape with the raider.

Poison pills as defensive tactics have become a cornerstone of corporate board defensive tactics since 1985. However, neither the Delaware court, nor a federal district court has provided clues as to how long a board can maintain a pill against an inadequate bid. After twenty-five years, the Delaware Chancery Court, has recently, in Air Products and Chemicals, Inc[23] shed light by providing specific criteria to look at. While the court recognized that the board ability to maintain the pill is not absolute, the court highlights the elements that the judge should take into account in making a proper determination:

- Board acting in good faith;
- Board relying upon outside independent financial advisors in making its decision;
- Board determination supported by the company strategic plan, prepared in normal course of business;
- Board composed in majority by independent directors;
- The raider offer is final.

Whenever those elements are found in the case, the Delaware court would approve the maintenance of the board poison pill deterrence.

Mostly, poison pills are referred to as whether "flip-in" pills or "flip-over" pills. The two are quite different.

- Flip-In Pills

In a flip-in pill, shareholders other than the hostile bidder are allowed to acquire, with the approval of the board, additional shares of the target corporation at a significant discount[24] of their current market value. When these shareholders exercise their right, the corporate equity became significantly diluted, rendering the takeover more expensive.

- Flip-Over Pills

Flip-over pill is somehow different from the flip-in in that the acquisition of additional shares by non-bidder shareholder occurs after the bidder has already takeover the target corporation. The flip-over pill, which exists in the target corporation bylaws are triggered by the target board reinforcing the position of the preexisting shareholders in the target equity. The effect is almost the same as with the flip-in pill, the target equity is diluted. The flip-over pill reserves the triggering power to the target board discretion.

Poison pill constitutes a challenge to the aim of corporate governance, which is to protect the interests of the shareholders at any lifetime of the company, including in the face of a hostile takeover. That is because poison pill is often installed through the board's action without shareholders' involvement, at the first place. In a string of poison pills decisions rendered by the Delaware courts, it is obvious that a poison pill, if properly structured, adopted, and administered continues to be one of the most powerful and effective tools at the hand of the board of directives to withstand a hostile takeover. The treat becomes obvious with the recognition, by the Delaware court, of new types of poison pills such as the ones in the Selectica[25] and the Airgas cases.[26]

In both cases, the boards have installed as a protective financial buffer to protect the Net Operating Losses (NOLs) have accumulated because of the recent financial crisis.

As a general corporate tax rule, when a corporation acquires the stock of another corporation in a tax-free restructuring, the acquired corporation shareholders change, but under certain requirements, the tax attributes of the acquired corporation pass to the acquirer corporation.[27] However, when the restructuring leads to a more- than-50 percentage point change in the ownership of the acquirer relative to the "old acquired corporation" the tax code puts some limitations under IRC section 382. The NOL carryover that may be utilized each year is limited to the long-term tax-exempt rate multiplied by the stock value of the loss corporation immediately prior to the ownership change. To avoid such occurrence, some boards are installing poison pills to that aim.

These two cases illustrate the boards' concerns:

5.5.2 The Staggered Board Techniques

The staggered boards constitute another defensive tactic that might limit the shareholders power over the corporation. The power of staggered board is even enhanced when couple with poison pill. The power of the staggered board has been expounded by Lucian Bebchuk, who argued that, in light of the empirical data, shareholders in companies with staggered board never receive higher premiums relative to shareholders in companies without staggered board.[28] In general, a staggered board provides for three classes of directors with only one class of directors up for election each year, making it difficult for a bidder to win annual proxy contest. A bidder facing a resistant board, which has a poison pill in place, would need to win at least two subsequent proxy fights in order to replace the fighting current board. The process is time consuming and costly. In most cases, the bidder would resist to pursue with the offer, leaving powerless shareholders at the mercy of their current management. The power inherent in this type of defense is felt two-fold: (i) the bidder must wage two successful proxy contests separated by a year, and (ii) the bidder's shareholders must endure a prolonged period of depressed stock price while the bidder negotiates the merger. Therefore, shareholder activists and other institutional shareholders oppose classified boards because they come to see them as symbol of management entrenchment. A study conducted by RiskMetrics Group's Governance Indicators (GRID), in 2010, reveals that a straight correlation between a classified board structure and a reduction in firm value.

The following cases illustrate the evolution of the staggered board within the Delaware Courts.

Schnell v. Chris-Craft Industries, Inc.

The facts of the case can be summarized as follow:

- After the shareholders of Chris-Craft Industries express their intent to replace the incumbent directors because of the corporation's poor performance.
- The directors voted to advance the date of the annual shareholder meeting by a month. The directors moved the annual meeting up from January to December, making it harder for stockholders to make travel arrangements (and therefore show up to vote to kick out the directors).
- Some shareholders including Schnell sued on the ground that the directors changed the date of the meeting for frustrating a shareholder vote on the issue of replacing the directors, in violation of their fiduciary duties.

In fact, the DGCL enables the board of directors to reschedule the shareholders' annual meeting so long it provides 60-day notice.

Chris-Craft board complied with the 60-day notice required by the DGCL.

- The Trial Court found for the directors.
- The shareholders appealed. The Trial Court found that the directors' actions were designed to obstruct the shareholders' efforts to gain control of the corporation. However, the Court declined to force the directors to reschedule the meeting.
- The Delaware Supreme Court reversed.

The Delaware Supreme Court found that even though the directors strictly complied with Delaware law, it was inequitable for them to profit from their shady decision. The Court found that (i) mere compliance with the letter of the law does not validate an otherwise inequitable action; (ii) Directors may not use the corporate machinery in such a way as to frustrate dissident shareholders' legitimate attempts to exercise their voting rights.

Blasius Industry Inc. v. Atlas Corp.

The facts of case can be summarized as follow:

- After acquiring 9.1% of the outstanding shares of Blasius Industries, Atlas Corp. announced its intention to explore the possibility of acquiring control of the company and implementing a restructuring.
- Acting through a subsidiary, Atlas submitted to Blasius a "precatory resolution" indicating its intention to expand the board from seven to fifteen members and to appoint enough directors to control a majority of the new board.
- The directors of Blasius responded by adding two members to the board, thereby preventing Atlas Corp. from installing a majority in the proposed fifteen-member board. Atlas challenged the decision on the ground that it was an improper exercise of the directors' power.

The Chancery Court ruled that because the appointment of directors lies at the foundation of the agency relationship between shareholders and the board, the directors of a corporation should not have the power to take any action whose intended effect is to entrench the incumbent directors' control of the board. The Court ruled that even though the board acted "in a good faith effort to protect its incumbency, not selfishly, but in order to thwart implementation of the recapitalization that it feared, reasonably, would cause great injury to the Company," it could not, consistent with its fiduciary duty, act "for the primary purpose of preventing or impeding an unaffiliated majority of shareholders from expanding the board and electing a new majority."

MM Companies, Inc. v. Liquid Audio, Inc.

The salient facts of the case can be summed up as follow:

- MM Companies, Inc., which owned approximately 7% of Liquid Audio's common stock, notified Liquid Audio's board that it was willing to acquire Liquid Audio for approximately $30.00 per share.
- The board rejected the offer. Soon after, in June 2002, MM Companies, Inc., began to solicit proxies for the annual shareholder meeting scheduled for July 1, 2002.
- MM Companies Inc. sought two things: (i) the election of its two nominees for the directorships on Liquid Audio's staggered board, and (ii) the increase of the Board size from five to nine, and to fill those positions with its own nominees in order to control the new board.
- Before the meeting, Liquid Audio announced a stock-for-stock merger with Alliance Entertainment Corp. and postponed the annual meeting. In response to a suit by MM Companies Inc., the Chancery Court ordered Liquid Audio to hold its annual meeting in late September 2002.
- On August 23, 2002, Liquid Audio announced that its board of directors had amended its bylaws to increase the size of the board to seven members and that the board had appointed two persons to fill the newly created seats on the board.
- MM Companies Inc. then amended an earlier suit to allege that the August expansion of the board from five to seven members and the appointment of two new members by the incumbent board violated the shareholders voting rights and stood in violation of the Chancery the principles as developed and articulated under both Blasius and Unocal.

The Court rejected MM amended claim, finding that the board expansion "did not impact the shareholder vote or the shareholders' choices in any significant way."

The Supreme Court of Delaware reversed the Court of Chancery's decision. The Supreme Court ruled that the Unocal standard of review must be applied whenever a board adopts any defensive measure "in response to some threat to corporate policy and effectiveness which touches upon issues of control."

The Court found that:

This case presents a paragon of when the compelling justification standard of Blasius must be applied within Unocal's requirement that any defensive measure be proportionate and reasonable in relation to the threat posed. The Unocal standard of review applies because the Liquid Audio board's action was a "defensive measure taken in response to some threat to corporate policy and effectiveness which touches upon issues of control."

Further, the Supreme Court ruled that the compelling justification standard of Blasius had to be applied within an application of the Unocal standard to that specific defensive measure because the primary purpose of the Board's action was to interfere with or impede the effective exercise of the shareholder franchise in a contested election for directors.

5.5.3 *Shareholders Derivative Litigation: A Hurdle race*

To establish a shareholder's derivative action, plaintiff must (i) establish a standing; (ii) either make a pre-suit demand on the corporation board of directors or allege demand futility; (iii) adequacy of the demand. Each step requires a herculean effort that the Delaware court itself recognized the heaviness and the unlikelihoodness of success.

(i) Standing

In general, or under the Federal Rule of Civil Procedure, the plaintiff must meet the requirements of FRCP 23.1, which provides, in pertinent part that:

In a derivative action,...the complaint ...shall allege... that the plaintiff was a shareholder or member at the time of the transaction of which the plaintiff complains or that the plaintiff's share or membership thereafter devolved on the plaintiff by operation of law.

The Delaware procedural law is even more restrictive as it requires that plaintiff remain stockholder throughout the litigation. Otherwise, plaintiff loses the standing to pursuit a derivative action. However, despite the statutory contemporaneous stock ownership under 8 Del. C. Par. 327, Rule 23.1 of the FRCP allows stockholders who purchase shares after the alleged wrongful conduct began to pursue their claims if the alleged wrong is a continuing one and has not been consummated. To determine whether a wrong complained of is a continuing wrong; courts examine "when the specific acts of alleged wrongdoing occur, and not when their effect is felt."

(ii) Demand or futility of demand

Rule 23.1 requires that the shareholder (plaintiff) makes a pre-suit demand to the corporation's board of directors or allege that such a demand is futile. In general, shareholder, through a derivative action would either challenge the action taken by the board or the board inaction. The Delaware courts have developed two different set of standard depending on whether the plaintiff is challenging the board's action or inaction.

In any event, the Delaware Court of Chancery has identified the factors that plaintiff must satisfy for its claim to qualified as a demand. In Yav. v. Talley, the Chancery Court has held:

To constitute a demand, a communication must specifically state: (i) the identity of the alleged wrongdoers, (ii) the wrongdoing they allegedly perpetrated and the resultant injury to the corporation, and (iii) the legal action the shareholder wants the board to take on the corporation's behalf.

The requirement is stringent, as the Delaware Courts have held that the ambiguity of the plaintiff's communication to the corporation should be constructed against the finding that demand was made. Further, the Delaware Supreme court has held that a stockholder who makes a demand on the board of directors waives his right to claim that demand would be futile. Likewise, when the board of directors has rejected a plaintiff demand, the plaintiff is barred from alleging demand futility.

Once a plaintiff has made a proper and adequate demand, the board of directors should have sufficient and adequate time to respond to the demand whether by taking the plaintiff requested action or by rejecting the demand. If the board of directors decides to reject the demand, plaintiff chances to process are slim because the best judgment rule would shield and protect the board decision, unless, the plaintiff alleges particularized facts to establish the wrongness of the board's rejection. Due to the hurdles to succeed an adequate demand, plaintiffs, in derivative action have a tendency to commence an action without making a demand at all. To that end, plaintiff must show that director's conduct was so egregious on its face that board approval cannot meet the test of business judgment, and a substantial likelihood of director's liability therefore exists. The Delaware Supreme Court has developed the test for evaluating the futility of demand whether when the plaintiff challenges the board's action or the board failure to act.

- The Plaintiff Challenge of the Board Action(s)

When plaintiff challenges the board's action, the Delaware Courts apply a two-prong test developed in Aronson v. Lewis to assess demand futility. In that case, the Delaware Supreme Court held:

In determining demand futility, the Court of Chancery in the proper exercise of its discretion must decide whether, under the particularized facts alleged, a reasonable doubt is created that (i) the directors are disinterested and independent, or (ii) the challenged transaction was otherwise the product of a valid exercise of business judgment.

More, plaintiff must establish that demand is excused or futile as to each separate claim.

Aronson First Prong
Under each prong of the Aronson, plaintiff must plead particularized facts creating a reasonable doubt that (i) the directors are disinterested and independent, or (ii) that the transaction was a valid exercise of the board business judgment. Directors' interest would exist if directors appear on both sides of a transaction or expect to derive any personal financial benefit from it in the sense of self-dealing. Plaintiff alleging directors' lack of independence must establish particularized facts that support that through personal or other relationships, the directors are beholden to the controlling person.

Aronson Second Prong
Under the second prong of Aronson, plaintiff must plead particularized facts sufficient to raise (i) a reason to doubt that the board's action was taken honestly and in good faith, or (ii) a reason to doubt that the board was adequately informed in making the decision. Meeting the second prong requirement is often an insurmountable hurdle as the Delaware Supreme Court has usually maintained that:

Approval of a transaction by a majority of independent, disinterested directors almost always bolsters a presumption that the business judgment rule attaches to transactions approved by a board of directors that are latter attacked on ground of lack of due care.

- The Plaintiff Challenge of the Board Inaction

When the board has not taken any action concerning the attacked transaction, the Delaware Courts assess the futility of demand under the Rales standard. That is, plaintiff must plead particularized facts that show that directors completely and utterly failed to even attempt to meet their duties. The burden is heavy and often insurmountable.

(iii) Adequacy of the Claim

To pursue a derivative action, a plaintiff who has met the standing and the demand requirement, must also fairly and adequately represent the interests of all stockholders. Rules 23.1 provides that:

The derivative action may not be maintained if it appears that the plaintiff does not fairly and adequately represent the interests of the shareholders or members similarly situated in enforcing the right of the corporation.

However, the Delaware courts have also recognized that derivative actions could be maintained even if the representative stockholder did not have the support of a majority of the corporation's stockholders. In Emerald Partners, the Chancery Court has held that:

Among the elements which the courts have evaluated in considering whether the derivative plaintiff meets Rule 23.1's representation requirements are economic antagonisms between representative and class; the remedy sought by the plaintiff in the derivative action; indications that the named plaintiff was not the driving force behind the litigation; plaintiff's unfamiliarity with the litigation; other litigation pending between the plaintiff and defendants; the relative magnitude of plaintiff's personal interest as compared to his interest in the derivative action itself; plaintiff's vindictiveness toward the defendants and, finally, the degree of support plaintiff was receiving from the shareholders he purported to represent.

(iv) Disclosure of Materials

It is extremely difficult for a shareholder-plaintiff to succeed at trial.
Disclosure: contrary to Martin Gelter allegations, the pre-trial discovery is almost not granted. Shareholder-plaintiffs are not entitled to discovery (even limited) to assist their compliance with the particularized pleading requirement of Rule 23.1 in a case of demand refusal, nor in demand excused cases. Rather, the Delaware courts have reiterated that shareholder-plaintiffs should avail themselves of the tools at hand when filing derivative actions. Indeed, section 220 of the DGCL allows

shareholder-plaintiffs to inspect the minutes, records, and other corporate books. More, the Delaware courts have always asserted that:

There is variety of public sources from which the details of a corporate act may be discovered, including the media and governmental agencies such as the Securities and Exchange Commission.

Paradoxically, in the Citigroup case, where the shareholder-plaintiff claims were that the Citigroup board ignored a number of "red flags" that signaled likely problems in the subprime mortgage market in pursuit of short-term profits. The "red flags" referred to by the plaintiffs were events from May 27, 2005, to October 18, 2007, including a *New York Times* article warning of a speculative bubble in the housing market, the decline and failure of certain subprime lenders, Freddie Mac's announcement that it would refinance borrowers unable to afford their resetting adjustable-rate mortgages, credit rating agency downgrades of subprime bonds, and warnings of spreading mortgage defaults.

The Court, here, found that red flags raised in the public information did not constitute particularized facts susceptible to establish the board failure to monitor.

The "red flags" in the Complaint amount to little more than portions of public documents that reflected the worsening conditions in the subprime mortgage market and in the economy generally.

However, a narrow discovery exception may exist in case where a special litigation committee was set up to look over the shareholder-plaintiff claim. Under what is referred to as the "Zapata" requirement, the corporation should bear the burden of proving independence, good faith, and reasonable investigation of its committee, rather than presuming independence, good faith, and reasonableness. The court still may exercise its own (discretionary) business judgment before granting such a narrowed discovery exception. In most of the cases, the courts have rejected the shareholder-plaintiff requests.

5.5.4 A New Standard of Liability for the Board

Enhancing the standard of liability of gatekeepers such as accountants, auditors, analyst, and notation agencies is a path to consider if the US wants to avoid repetitive financial market scandals, cooking of books, and other destruction of evidence by auditors. The cross-selling of consulting services by auditing firms, the credit rating agencies, the analysts, coupled with the roll-over practice between the federal agency employees in SEC, the Federal Reserve, and other agencies justify and support a call for enhanced standard of liability pursuant to gatekeepers. Moreover, the auditing and rating agency industries have been characterized as super-concentrated by the Government Accountability Office (GAO). Facing new series of regulations, the gatekeepers remain even in size despite the request for fact that is more laborious checking. The tendency will last as the Public Company Accounting Oversight Board has recognized, in 2008, that its quality controls are inadequate. To protect shareholders and the financial markets' trust, the US government can do three things (i) to enhance the standard of liability, (ii) to use its constitutional power as a market participant to shift public contracts to mid-size firms, or (iii) back up the EU Commission effort to dismantle the big four, which become too big to control. The European Union Commission is considering a "Regulation" that could eradicate the conflicts of interest under which the big four operates. The draft of the regulation, in part, says: "audit firms of significant dimension should not be allowed to undertake other services unconnected to their statutory audit function such as consultancy and advisory services." Whether it is the European Union or tomorrow China, and the G-20, the restructuring proposal would allow other small- and mid-size audit firms penetrate the auditing market and provide quality-oriented audit, rather than the complacent unqualified opinions we become so accustomed to.

Legal Insights

I. *Fiduciary Duties*

A. Brehm v. Eisner (In re Walt Disney Co. Derivative Litig.)—906 A.2d 27 (Del. 2006):

The good faith required of a corporate fiduciary includes not simply the duties of care and loyalty, but all actions required by a true faithfulness and devotion to the interests of the corporation and its shareholders. A failure to act in good faith may be shown, for instance, where the fiduciary intentionally acts with a purpose other than that of advancing the best interests of the corporation, where the fiduciary acts with the intent to violate applicable positive law, or where the fiduciary intentionally fails to act in the face of a known duty to act, demonstrating a conscious disregard for his duties.

Facts:

- In August 1995, Michael Ovitz ("Ovitz") and The Walt Disney Company ("Disney" or the "Company") entered into an employment agreement under which Ovitz would serve as President of Disney for five years.
- Ovitz lacked experience managing a diversified public company. He was a friend of Eisner, Disney's Chairman, who alone negotiated Ovitz's Employment Agreement with Disney, which was approved by Disney's Board of Directors
- Fourteen months after he commenced employment, Ovitz was terminated without cause, resulting in a severance payout to Ovitz valued at approximately $130 million.
- In January 1997, several Disney shareholders brought derivative actions in the Court of Chancery, on behalf of Disney, against Ovitz and the directors of Disney who served at the time of the events complained of.
- Disney shareholders claimed that the $130 million severance payout was the product of fiduciary duty and contractual breaches by Ovitz, and breaches of fiduciary duty by Ovitz and the Disney directors, and a waste of assets.
- The Court of Chancery ruled that the director defendants did not breach their fiduciary duties or commit waste.
- Disney shareholders appealed before the Delaware Supreme Court, which affirmed the judgment.
- The Court held that no reasonably prudent fiduciary in the president's position would have unilaterally called a board meeting to force the corporation's chief executive officer to reconsider his termination and the terms thereof, with that reconsideration for the benefit of shareholders and potentially to the president's detriment.
- The decisions to approve the president's employment agreement, to hire him as president, and then to terminate him on a non-fault basis were protected business judgments, made without any violations of fiduciary duty. Having so concluded, it was unnecessary to reach the shareholders' contention that the directors were required to prove that the payment of severance was entirely fair. Because the shareholders failed to show that, the approval of the no-fault termination terms of the employment agreement was not a rational business decision, their corporate waste claim failed.

B. Malone vs Brincat

Whenever directors communicate publicly or directly with shareholders about the corporation's affairs, with or without a request for shareholder action, directors have a fiduciary duty to shareholders to exercise due care, good faith, and loyalty. When directors communicate publicly or directly with shareholders about corporate matters, the sine qua non of directors' fiduciary duty to shareholders is honesty.

The board of directors was authorized to adopt a "poison pill." The decision to adopt a poison pill shall be evaluated under the business judgment rule. The business judgment rule is the standard by which to evaluate the adoption of a defensive mechanism adopted to ward off possible future advances.

Facts:

- The Board of Directors of Household Int'l Inc., adopted the Preferred Share Purchase Rights Plan, (Plan), as a preventative measure against future takeover attempts.
- Subsequently, D-K-M and its Chairman, Moran brought a lawsuit.
- The Plan provides that Household Int'l Inc. common stockholders were entitled to the issuance of one Right per common share under two triggering conditions. The triggers were, first, a tender offer for 30% of the shares and second, the acquisition of 20% of the shares by any single entity or group.
- Once triggered, the Right authorizes the holder to purchase $200 of common stock of the offerer or purchaser for $100 thereby causing massive dilution of the value of the aggressor's shares.
- Prior to the triggering event, the right is automatically fixed to the shares and cannot be traded separately form the shares.
- At issue was whether the business judgment rule is the standard to be applied to the adoption of the Plan by the board.
- The Court held that the ultimate response to an actual takeover bid must be judged by the Directors actions at the time they made the decision bearing in their mind the fundamental duties to the corporation and its shareholders.
- Further, added the Court, the Directors cannot arbitrarily reject the offer because they would still be held to the business judgment rule.
- Whenever directors communicate publicly or directly with shareholders about the corporation's affairs, with or without a request for shareholder action, directors have a fiduciary duty to shareholders to exercise due care, good faith, and loyalty. When directors communicate publicly or directly with shareholders about corporate

matters, the sine qua non of directors' fiduciary duty to shareholders is honesty.

II. *Best Judgment Rules Standards*

A. The Revlon standard: When a takeover is inevitable, the directors' duty is to achieve the best price for the shareholder.

Facts.

- Pantry Pride's CEO approached Revlon's CEO and offered a $40–42 per share price for Revlon or $45 if it had to be a hostile takeover.
- The CEO's had personal differences, and the court noted this as a potential motivation for Revlon to turn elsewhere.
- Revlon's directors met and decided to adopt a poison pill plan and to repurchase five million of Revlon's shares.
- Pantry Pride countered with a $47.50 price, which pushed Revlon to repurchase ten million shares with senior subordinated notes.
- Pantry Pride continued to increase their bids, and Revlon decided to seek another buyer in Forstmann.
- Revlon offered $56.25 with the promise to increase the bidding further if another bidding topped that price. Instead, Revlon made an agreement to have Forstmann pay $57.25 per share subject to certain restrictions such as a $25 million cancellation fee for Forstmann and a no-shop provision.
- MacAndrews & Forbes Holdings, Inc., sought to enjoin the agreement because it was not in the best interests of the shareholders.
- Defendants argued that they needed to also consider the best interests of the noteholders.
- The issue was whether Revlon's agreement with Forstmann should be enjoined because it was not in the best interests of the shareholders.
- The Court of Chancery issued an injunction in favor of the shareholders.
- The Delaware Supreme Court affirmed the lower court's decision to enjoin the agreement.
- That under all the circumstances, the directors allowed considerations other than the maximization of shareholder profit to affect their judgment, and followed a course that ended the auction for Revlon, absent court intervention, to the ultimate detriment of its shareholders.

- Revlon's directors owed a fiduciary duty to the shareholders and the corporation, but once it was evident that a third party would buy Revlon, the directors had a duty solely to the shareholders to get the best price for their shares.

B. Unocal standard: Unocal Corp., appealed the lower court decision that prevented Unocal from excluding Mesa Petroleum Co., from participating in Defendant's self-tender for its own shares.

Facts.

- Mesa Petroleum was a corporation led by a well-known corporate raider.
- Mesa Petroleum offered a two-tier tender offer wherein the first tier would allow for shareholders to sell at $54 per share and the second tier would be subsidized by securities that the court equated with "junk bonds."
- The threat therefore was that shareholders would rush to sell their shares for the first tier because they did not want to be subject to the reduced value of the back-end value of the junk securities.
- Unocal Corp's directors met to discuss their options and came up with an alternative that would have Unocal Corporation repurchased their own shares at $72 each.
- Unocal Directors decided to exclude Mesa Petroleum from the tender offer because it was counterintuitive to include the shareholder who initiated the conflict.
- The lower court held that Unocal corp. could not exclude a shareholder from a tender offer.
- The issue is whether Unocal Corp. can exclude Mesa Petroleum Co. from participating in Unocal's self-tender.
- The court held that Unocal Corp. could exclude Mesa Petroleum Co. from its repurchase of its own shares.
- Unocal Corp. directors have a duty to protect the shareholders and the corporations, and one of the harms that can befall a company is a takeover by a shareholder who is offering an inadequate offer. The directors' decision to prevent an offer such as the one at issue should be subjected to an enhanced scrutiny since there is a natural conflict when the directors are excluding a party from acquiring a majority control. In this case, the directors met the burden. There was evidence to support that the company was in reasonable danger. the outside directors approved of their self-tender, the offer by Mesa

Petroleum Co. included the junk bonds, the value of each share was more than the proposed $54 per share, and Plaintiff was well known as a corporate raider.

Note: The burden of proof was on the directors to prove that there was a legitimate business interest at stake to rebut the presumption of their conflicting interest in denying the takeover. This was well established, but the allowance by the court to allow the directors to deny Mesa Petroleum Co. from participating in the resulting repurchase was new ground.

C. The Paramount standard: A merger agreement between a target company and an acquiring company that restricts the target company's directors from upholding their fiduciary duties owed to their shareholders is invalid.

Facts.

- Paramount was looking for possible merger or acquisition targets in order to remain competitive in their field.
- The CEO of Paramount had a meeting with the CEO of Viacom wherein they discussed Paramount merging into Viacom. The discussions hit a dead end until QVC sought to acquire Paramount.
- The discussions between QVC and Paramount were renewed, and the parties entered a merger agreement that had several defensive measures to prevent other companies, namely QVC, from bidding against Viacom.
- There was a no-shop provision that prevented Paramount from soliciting other bidders; a termination fee provision that paid Viacom $100 million if they were eventually outbid; and a stock option provision that allowed Viacom to purchase 19.9% of Paramount's shares at $69.14 per share.
- The stock option provision also allowed Viacom to pay for the stock in subordinated notes or Viacom could elect to get a cash payout for the difference between the option price and market price.
- The stock option was significant because Paramount's shares rose sharply and would have led at one point to a $500 million payout to Viacom if the merger fell through.
- QVC started bidding against Viacom's offer, which forced Viacom to renegotiate with Paramount to raise their offer—although the defensive measures were never renegotiated.

- QVC raised their offer even further, but Paramount believed that the offer was too conditional (similar to Viacom's offer, it was two-tiered), and the board still felt that the merger was not in the company's best interests.
- Therefore, the Paramount board turned down a QVC offer that could have been about $1 billion more than Viacom's offer. In the lower court, Plaintiffs successfully enjoined Defendants from carrying out the merger agreement.
- The issue is whether the Paramount board violated their fiduciary duty to shareholders by not fully considering the QVC offer.
- The Delaware Supreme Court held that the merger between Defendants should be enjoined, and that the merger agreement between Paramount and Viacom was invalid.
- Paramount Communications, Inc. et al. argued that they were under no obligation to seek the maximum value for shareholders under the Revlon rule because there was no breakup of the company, but the court determined that the company was shifting its control to another entity and therefore the sale of Paramount reached the point to where the prime concern for the Paramount directors was to maximize shareholder value.
- Paramount was under no contractual obligation to avoid discussions with QVC because the merger agreement between Viacom and Paramount was invalid. Paramount could not contract to remove their fiduciary duties to shareholders, and the defensive provisions had that effect.

Notes

1. Moleney v. Brincat, 722 A.2d 5, 10 (Del. 1998).
2. Christopher M. Bruner, Power and Purpose in the Anglo-American corporation, Virginia Journal of International Law, Volume 50, Issue 3, p. 599.
3. Francis v. New Jersey Bank, 432 A.2d 814 (N.J. 1981).
4. In Re Walt Disney Co. Derivative Litigation (Del. Ch. 2003).
5. In Re Walt Disney Co. v. Derivative Litigation (Disney IV), 906 A.2d 27, 63–68.
6. Brehm v. Eisner, 906 A.2d 27, 64 (Del. 2006).
7. Malone v. Brincat, 722 A.2d 5 (Del. 1998).
8. Unocal Corp. v. Mesa Petroleum Co., 493 A.2d 946 (Del. 1985).

9. Smith v. Van Gorkom, 488 A.2d 858 (Del. 1985).
10. Revlon Inc., v. MacAndrews & Forbes Holding Inc., 506 A.2d 173 (Del. 1985).
11. Idem, reference # 24.
12. Paramount Communications, Inc. v. QVC Network, Inc. 637 A.2d (Del. 1994).
13. To satisfy this standard, the directors must prove that they were informed and acting in good faith.
14. The second condition requires the Board prove two things: (1) that the response was not "coercive" or "preclusive", and (2) the response was within a range of reasonableness.
15. Phelps Dodge v. Cyprus Amax Minerals Co. C.A N0. 17,398 (Del. Ch. Sept. 27, 1999).
16. Mills Acquisition co. v. Macmillan, Inc. 559 A.2d 1261 (Del. 1989).
17. Omnicare3 v. NCS Healthcare Inc., 818 A.2d 914 (Del. 2003).
18. Franklin R. Edwards, in US Corporate Governance: What Went Wrong and Can It Be Fixed?, Federal Reserve Bank of Chicago Conference, Nov. 1, 2003, p. 17.
19. In Re Emerging Communications Shareholders Litigation (Del. Ch., May 3, 2004).
20. In Re Citigroup, Inc., (Del. Ch. 2009).
21. The term "poison pill" comes from the domain of espionage and refers to the cyanide pill spies were instructed to swallow rather than face capture. In the field of corporate takeover, poison pill is a device used by a corporate board to resist inadequate hostile takeover.
22. Moran v. Household International Inc., 500 A.2d 1346 (Del. 1985).
23. Moran v. Household International Inc., 500 A.2d 1346 (Del. 1985).
24. Often the discount is within the range of 50–60%.
25. Versata Enterprises v. Selectica, Inc. (Del. 2010).
26. Air Prods & Chemicals, Inc., Airgas, Inc., (Del. Ch. Feb. 15, 2011).
27. IRC sections 269, and 381–384.
28. Lucian A. Bebchuk, The Powerful Antitakeover Force of Staggered Board, Stanford Law Review, 2002, p. 890.

CHAPTER 6

Shareholders Actions

6.1 General

Shareholders may enforce their rights against the corporation (or its officers and directors) in one of two ways: direct actions and/or derivative actions. A direct shareholder claim is one in which the shareholder sues on his own behalf for damages alleged to have harmed the shareholder individually, and not simply harmed the shareholder because he owns a portion of the company.[1] Conversely, a shareholder derivative action is a lawsuit brought by a corporation shareholder against the directors, management, and/or other shareholders of the corporation, for a failure by management.

6.2 Types of Actions

6.2.1 Shareholders Direct Action

If the plaintiffs had suffered special injury, then the plaintiffs could sue directly, even if the same wrong injured the corporation as well. A stockholder suffered injury when its contractual rights were breached.

Delaware Supreme Court decisions had used the concept of special injury to determine when a plaintiff could sue directly.[2] A special injury was defined as a wrong—separate and distinct from that suffered by other shareholders ... or a wrong involving a contractual right of a shareholder.

F. Lessambo, *U.S. Mergers and Acquisitions*,
https://doi.org/10.1007/978-3-030-85735-6_6

6.2.2 *Derivative Claims*

Derivative claims are another category of claims that investors in Delaware entities bring. The concept of the derivative action as two actions in one bridged the gap by permitting the stockholder to sue the corporation's managers for failing to pursue a claim against a third party belonging to the corporation. The seminal decision was Forbes v. Whitlock, 3 Edw. Ch. 446 (N.Y. Ch. 1841). There, a third party defendant sold property to a corporation in return for stock. The plaintiffs sued in their capacity as stockholders, seeking to set aside the contract on grounds of fraud and to recover damages for its breach.

[T]he court viewed the situation as one in which all rights vested in the corporation to which the covenants ran.... Only the rights of the corporate personality were at stake and those must be asserted in the corporate name.

... Thus, to avoid what was vaguely referred to as endless difficulty and embarrassment, If the corporate entity concept was employed to defeat a shareholder's action. But plaintiffs also sought to hold defendant for misconduct in the office of treasurer to which he succeeded as a result of his sale of property for corporate stock. To this extent, the bill presented managerial abuse, but the court applied its conceptualism to this part of the case as well.

Subsequent New York decisions built on Forbes to develop the idea that when a stockholder plaintiff sues, he sues in a derivative capacity and asserts a corporate cause of action. Any claim belonging to the corporation may, in appropriate circumstances, be asserted in a derivative action, including claims that do—and claims that do not—involve corporate mismanagement or breach of fiduciary duty.[3]

By enforcing the demand doctrine through the heightened pleading requirements of Rule 23.1, a derivative characterization guarantee[s] that the statutory power of directors to manage the legal affairs of the company [is] not disregarded except when necessary to serve the policy purpose justifying the recognition of the derivative suit in the first instance.[4]

6.2.3 Shareholders Dual Actions

- To determine whether a claim has dual characteristics, Delaware decisions have used the Tooley test. The first prong asks who suffered the alleged injury, the partnership or the limited partners individually. In cases addressing the distinction between derivative and direct claims, this is often as far as the assessment of the injury goes. However, a more realistic evaluation takes the additional step of recognizing that a wrongful third party transfer operates differently than a wrongful insider transfer. A wrongful third party transfer takes value out of the entity and away from the existing entity claimants. A wrongful insider transfer also takes value from the entity, but in doing so, it reallocates value among the existing entity claimants. All of the claimants suffer a proportionate loss according to the priority of their claims, but the insider receives an offsetting benefit that exceeds the insider's share of the loss. In reality, the insider is not injured at all. The insider gains at the expense of the other investors. The net effect is to extract value from the unaffiliated investors for the benefit of the insider.

  When the insider transfer involves the issuance of stock, Delaware cases have recognized the dual nature of the injury and the separate harm inflicted on the non-participating stockholders through the extraction of value.
- The second prong of Tooley asks who would receive the benefit of any recovery or other remedy, the partnership or the limited partners individually. Just as the injury in this case operated at both the entity and the investor levels, so can the remedy.

6.3 Types of Reliefs

6.3.1 Motion for Summary Judgment

In order to prevail on a motion for summary judgment, the moving party must show that no material facts are in dispute and that they are entitled to judgment as a matter of law.[5] In determining whether this burden is met, I must view the facts in the light most favorable to the non-moving party. Summary judgment may be denied if an action is not ripe.

In deciding whether an action is ripe for declaratory judgment, the benefits to be derived from issuing a declaratory judgment must be weighed against the court's desire to avoid advisory opinions.

A ripeness determination requires a common sense assessment of whether the interests of the party seeking immediate relief outweigh the concerns of the court "in postponing review until the question arises in some more concrete and final form." Generally, a dispute will be deemed ripe if "litigation sooner or later appears to be unavoidable and where the material facts are static." Conversely, a dispute will be deemed not ripe where the claim is based on "uncertain and contingent events" that may not occur, or where "future events may obviate the need" for judicial intervention.[6]

- In Moran v. Household International, Inc., for example, plaintiffs contested the "present effect" that Household's implementation of a stockholder rights plan was having on "their entitlement to receive and consider takeover proposals and to engage in a proxy fight for control of Household.[7]" In finding plaintiffs' challenge to the validity of the stockholders rights plan ripe for review, the Court reasoned that "the plaintiffs here are seeking a declaration that the Rights Plan, because of its deterrent features, presently affects shareholders' fundamental rights and is illegal under Delaware law."
- In KLM Royal Dutch Airlines v. Checchi,[8] the Court deemed ripe a challenge to a corporation's implementation of a rights plan where a stockholder had a preexisting option to purchase shares of the corporation in the future that, if exercised, would trigger the rights plan. Citing Moran, the Court found that the "poison pill presently interferes with [the stockholder's] contractual rights to exercise the option in the future."
- In Carmody v. Toll Brothers, Inc.,[9] the Court found a claim challenging the validity of a dead-hand provision in a stockholder rights plan to be ripe based on the reasoning in Moran.
- In Pontiac General Employees Retirement System v. Ballantine,[10] Vice Chancellor Laster found ripe for review a challenge to the implementation of a proxy put because of its "deterrent effect" on running a proxy contest.

6.3.2 Injunctive Relief

To obtain a preliminary injunction a plaintiff must demonstrate: (1) a reasonable probability of success on the merits; (2) that absent injunctive relief, they will suffer irreparable harm; and (3) that the balance of the parties' harms weighs in favor of injunctive relief. An injunction will not issue unless all three elements are satisfied.

Legal Insights

I. Carmody v. Toll Brothers, Inc. (Del. Ch. 1998)

Facts:

- Toll Brothers, Inc. concluded in the late 1990s that it had become an attractive takeover candidate.
- In June 1997, the company adopted a poison-pill defense plan (the Rights Plan). Toll Brothers was not facing a specific threat, but the company stated that it wanted to protect its shareholders from coercive or unfair tactics that might accompany a takeover bid.
- The Rights Plan granted options to all shareholders that would trigger the dilution of the company's stock if any acquiror obtained or made a tender offer to obtain 15% of Toll Brothers' stock.
- The Rights Plan was accompanied by a dead-hand provision, which stated that the Rights Plan could not be redeemed by anyone other than the current board members or their designated successors.
- Toll Brothers' certificate of incorporation did not provide that directors might have varying degrees of voting authority.
- A Toll Brothers shareholder sued the company and its board members, arguing that the dead-hand provision unlawfully restricted the power of future boards and was therefore invalid as ultra vires.
- The shareholder claimed in the alternative that the directors breached their duty of loyalty by approving the dead-hand provision because it violated the *Blasius* rule and the *Unocal* test.
- According to the complaint, the "dead hand" provision had a twofold practical effect:
  - First, it made an unsolicited offer for the company more unlikely by eliminating a proxy contest as a useful way for a hostile acquiror to gain control, because even if the acquiror won the contest, its newly elected director representatives could not redeem the Rights.

- Second, the "dead hand" provision disenfranchises, in a proxy contest, all shareholders that wished the company to be managed by a board empowered to redeem the Rights, by depriving those shareholders of any practical choice except to vote for the incumbent directors. Given these effects, the Shareholder claimed that the only purpose that the "dead hand" provision could serve was to discourage future acquisition activity by making any proxy contest to replace incumbent board members an exercise in futility.

- The board members moved to dismiss the complaint for failure to state a claim. They argued three reasons why the Chancery Court should dismiss the case:
  - *First*, they argue that the Shareholders claims were not ripe and could not become ripe for adjudication, unless and until (i) a specific acquisition was proposed to which the Continuing Directors object and (ii) the Continuing Directors refused to redeem the Rights so as to enable the shareholders to consider the acquisition proposal and decide whether or not to accept it.
  - *Second*, the board members contended that even if the claims were ripe, they must be dismissed under Chancery Court Rule 23.1, because the claims were derivative and the plaintiff had failed to make a pre-suit demand on the board or plead facts that would excuse a demand.
  - *Third*, the board members argued that in any event, the complaint failed to state a claim upon which relief could be granted, because the "dead hand" provision violated no duty imposed either by statute or corporate fiduciary principles.
- The issue was whether the Company's "dead hand" plan violated the Delaware General Corporation Law and/or the fiduciary duties of the directors who adopted the plan.
- The Chancery Court denied the Company's motion to dismiss, concluding that the complaint stated legally cognizable claims for relief. As the provision violated Del. Code tit. 8, § 141(a), (d) and amounted to breaches fiduciary duties, the complaint was ripe, and a pre-suit demand was not required.
- The Court found that the plan:

1. Conferred the power to redeem only upon some, but not all, of the directors, which transgressed the statutorily protected shareholder right to elect the directors who would be so empowered;
2. disenfranchised Carmody and other shareholders without a compelling justification;
3. Made a proxy contest "realistically unattainable," and;
4. Caused a current adverse impact. Because Carmody's claims were individual, not derivative, a pre-suit demand was not required and, if it were, grounds existed for excusal.

II. Corwin v. KKR Fin. Holdings LLC—125 A.3d 304 (Del. 2015):

When the stockholders of a corporation are fully informed of all material facts to a transaction, and the stockholders vote to approve the transaction, Delaware corporate law strives to give effect to business decisions approved by properly motivated directors and by informed, disinterested stockholders.
Facts:

- KKR bought all Financial Holdings' stock in a transaction formed as a merger.
- The merger was approved by a vote of fully informed, uncoerced, disinterested Financial Holdings stockholders.
- Corwin and other Financial Holdings stockholders sued to challenge the merger under the entire-fairness standard on the ground that KKR constituted a controlling stockholder of Financial Holdings because Financial Holdings was subject to the management of a KKR affiliate.
- KKR filed a motion to dismiss on the ground that KKR was not a controlling stockholder of Financial Holdings.
- The Chancery Court of Delaware granted the motion.
- Corwin and other Financial Holdings stockholders appealed.
- The Delaware Supreme Court was asked to adjudicate whether the Court of Chancery properly held that the complaint did not plead facts supporting an inference that KKR was a controlling stockholder of Financial Holdings.
- The Delaware Supreme Court affirmed the Chancery court holding:

The merger was not subject to the entire fairness standard of review as the acquiring limited partnership (LP) was not the acquired LLC's controlling stockholder, as LP owned less than 1% of LLC's stock, had no right to appoint any directors and had no contractual right to veto any board action. The investors knew that LLC's primary business was financing LP's leveraged buyout activities and that LLC was managed by LP's affiliate under a management agreement that could only be terminated if LLC paid a termination fee, and the LLC had assets controlled by its board, which could pursue any path its directors chose.

III. In re USG Corp. Stockholder Litigation, CONSOLIDATED C.A. No. 2018–0602-SG (Del. Ch. Aug. 31, 2020)

Where the stockholder-owners of a corporation are given an opportunity to approve a transaction, are fully informed of the facts material to the transaction, and where the transaction is not coercive, there is no agency problem for a court to review, and litigation challenging the transaction is subject to dismissal under the business judgment rule.
Facts:

- Gebr acquired USG Corporation, a building materials company. Knauf KG.
- USG's stockholders overwhelmingly approved the sale.
- Former USG stockholders filed a complaint alleging that USG's directors breached fiduciary duties in connection with USG's sale to Knauf, and sought monetary damages.
- Former USG stockholders alleged that USG's Board of Directors had reached a subjective belief that USG had an intrinsic value nearly 15% higher than the deal price, yet the directors failed to disclose this fact to USG's stockholders.
- USG Corporation filed a motion to dismiss, alleging that the Plaintiffs have failed to state a claim upon which relief can be granted against them. More, US Corporation alleged that due to an exculpation clause in USG's charter, the Former USG stockholders were required to demonstrate a breach of the duty of loyalty, or its doppelganger bad faith, to recover damages.
- As a rule, whenever defendants are exculpated from liability for damages by a provision in a charter (such as USG), absent breach of the duty of loyalty or bad faith, the Plaintiffs must plead facts that make it reasonably conceivable that the Defendants have acted with the requisite culpability.
- The Court found that Former USG stockholders failed to allege facts that could reasonably imply bad faith, and that the other facts

allegedly failed to state a claim of breach of the duty of loyalty or reasonably imply actions taken in bad faith.

- Accordingly, the USG Corporation motion to dismiss was granted.

Notes

1. J. Clark (2019): Direct and Derivative Shareholder Actions.
2. Lipton v. News Int'l, Plc, 514 A.2d 1075, 1079 (Del. 1986).
3. Stephen A. Radin, The Business Judgment Rule 3612 (6th ed. 2009) (quoting Midland Food Services., LLC v. Castle Hill Hldgs. V, LLC, 792 A.2d 920, 931 (Del. Ch.1999) (Strine, V.C.)).
4. Cochran v. Stifel Fin. Corp., 2000 WL 286,722, at *10 n.41 (Del. Ch. Mar. 8, 2000) (Strine, V.C.), reviewed in part on other grounds, 809 A.2d 555 (Del. 2002).
5. Ct. Ch. R. 56 (c).
6. XI Specialty Ins. Co. v. WMI Liquidating Trust, 93 A.3d 1208, 1217 (Del. 2014).
7. Moran v. Household Int'l, Inc., 490 A.2d 1059, 1072 (Del. Ch. 1985).
8. KLM Royal Dutch Airlines v. Checchi, 698 A.2d 380 (Del. Ch. 1997).
9. Carmody v. Toll Brothers, Inc., 723 A.2d 1180 (Del. Ch. 1998).
10. Pontiac General Employees Retirement System v. Ballantine, C.A. No. 9789-VCL at*72–77 (Del. Ch. Oct. 14, 2014).

CHAPTER 7

Proxy Contest, Staggered Boards

7.1 General

A proxy fight is an attempt by those not in control of a business to use the proxy method of voting to obtain a sufficient number of shareholder votes to gain control of the board of directors. The result is a change in the membership of the board, which then leads to a change in the management of the target company. The new board may approve of being acquired by the entity that initiated the proxy fight. The term proxy fight derived from the use of proxies. A proxy is the authorization of shareholders to vote their shares for them at the shareholders meeting. Since shares are voted at the shareholders meeting, and few shareholders bother to appear for that meeting, they instead grant a proxy to someone else who will be attending the meeting to vote their shares, such as the corporate secretary. It is the task of the acquirer to obtain the proxies for as many shares as possible, which it can then vote at the shareholders meeting.

Directors are elected once a year by the common shareholders, at the annual shareholders meeting that takes placed anywhere from two to five months following the end of a company's fiscal year-end. There may also be a special shareholders meeting for such issues as considering an acquisition offer, if a sufficient percentage of the voting shareholders request the meeting.

F. Lessambo, *U.S. Mergers and Acquisitions*,
https://doi.org/10.1007/978-3-030-85735-6_7

In a proxy fight, the acquirer and the target company use a variety of solicitation methods to influence shareholder votes for members of the board of directors. Shareholders must be sent a Schedule 14A, which contains a substantial amount of financial and other information about the target company; if the proxy fight is over a motion to sell the company, the schedule also includes the terms of the proposed acquisition. The basic steps in a proxy fight are:

- The acquirer hires a proxy solicitation firm, which is responsible for contacting shareholders.
- The proxy solicitor compiles a shareholder list and then contacts shareholders to state the case of the acquirer. In cases where shares are registered in the names of stock brokerages, the brokerages consult with the shareowners regarding the voting positions they will take.
- Individual shareholders or stock brokerages submit their votes to the entity designated to aggregate the information, such as a stock transfer agent or brokerage. These results are then forwarded to the corporate secretary of the target company just prior to the shareholders meeting. Votes may be scrutinized by proxy solicitors and challenged if votes are unclear, voted multiple times, or not signed.
- Directors are approved based on the votes received.

It can be quite difficult to gain the attention of shareholders, since the vast majority of them are completely apathetic in reviewing the options for directors. Instead, they usually agree to the director voting recommendations mailed to them without any examination of qualifications or underlying issues at all. The same level of apathy may apply to acquisition votes. However, a proxy fight might be favorable for the acquirer if the target company has been suffering from poor financial results, which might make shareholders restive. It is especially useful if the acquirer has a concrete proposal for turning around the business or shifting more cash to shareholders, such as through the use of asset sales, sale of the business, or increased dividends.

A proxy fight is not a high-probability option for an acquirer. However, it can still lead to changes, since the board of directors may be sufficiently scared by the proxy fight to enact a few changes to keep from triggering another proxy fight in the future. Examples of preventive changes include unusually large dividends and the sale of assets. In short, the acquirer must consider the low probability of acquiring through this approach and the costs incurred for proxy advisors, communications with shareholders, litigation, and proxy materials. The motivation for that fight is only peripherally about returning capital. It is more about power, and political competitiveness with shareholders, than about capital structure.

7.2 Proxy Fight and Shareholders' Motivation

Shareholders pursue proxy fight for three main reasons: (i) advocating greater social responsibility by corporations; (ii) enhancement of corporate governance; and (iii) as an investment strategy.

7.2.1 Advocating Corporate Social Responsibility

Corporate social responsibility (CSR) has become one of the standard business practices of our time. Corporate social responsibility (CSR) is a self-regulating business model that helps a company be socially accountable—to itself, its stakeholders, and the public. Being a socially responsible company can bolster a company's image and build its brand. Social responsibility empowers employees to leverage the corporate resources at their disposal to do well.

7.2.2 Enhancement of Corporate Governance

Proxy contests play a disciplinary role in aligning the interests of shareholders and managers. However, such a disciplinary role of proxy contests can be temporary and driven by the credibility of a proxy threat. Some activists may insist on a change in governance, such as the separation of the roles of chief executive officer and chair or new policies for director remuneration. An increase in the credibility of a proxy threat leads to more advantages, greater dividends, and fewer acquisitions. Incumbent managers reverse the policy changes at the expense of shareholders when the perceived credibility of a proxy threat is eliminated or subsides.[2]

7.2.3 Investment Strategy Tool

Many institutional investors (i.e., pension funds and insurance companies) that seek to match assets with liabilities over the long term are looking to invest in companies with well-established strategies and an established record of performance. Different investor groups may have different investment goals, time horizons, and priorities, which can create conflicting objectives and opinions among shareholders and complexity for the organization's senior leaders. They see proxy fight as a tool to change the ongoing strategy by replacing the incumbent directors with their own directors.

7.3 Proxy Disclosure Violation

When directors submit to the stockholders a transaction that requires stockholder approval (such as a merger, sale of assets, or charter amendment) or which requires a stockholder investment decision (such as tendering shares or making an appraisal election), the directors of a Delaware corporation are required to disclose fully and fairly all material information within the board's control.[3] A fact is material if there is a substantial likelihood that a reasonable shareholder would consider it important in deciding how to vote.[4] The inquiry does not require a substantial likelihood that [the] disclosure ... would have caused the reasonable investor to change his vote. Fiduciaries must also avoid misleading partial disclosures. Once directors begin to speak on a subject, they assume an obligation to provide the stockholders with an accurate, full, and fair characterization.

In Arnold II, the court held that the omission of key information about a competing bid was material even if the bid was highly speculative and contingent.

7.3.1 *Standards of Review*

The Business Judgment Rule

Delaware's default standard of review is the business judgment rule, a principle of non-review that reflects and promotes the role of the board of directors as the proper body to manage the business and affairs of the corporation. The rule presumes that in making a business decision the directors of a corporation acted on an informed basis, in good faith and in the honest belief that the action taken was in the best interests of the company. Unless one of its elements is rebutted, the court merely looks to see whether the business decision made was rational in the sense of being one logical approach to advancing the corporation's objectives.[5]

Only when a decision lacks any rationally conceivable basis will a court infer bad faith and a breach of duty.

- Burden of proof

In a transaction governed by the business judgment rule, the plaintiff has the burden at the pleadings stage to allege facts sufficient to rebut the presumptions of loyalty and good faith that protect the directors.

The Entire Fairness Review

Delaware most onerous standard of review—the entire fairness—applies when a plaintiff rebuts one or more of the presumptions of the business judgment rule; or when a plaintiff challenges the transaction between the corporation and its majority stockholder. The entire fairness test helps uncover situations where facially independent and disinterested directors have failed to act loyally and in good faith to protect the interests of the corporation and the stockholders as a whole and instead have given in to or favored the interests of the controller.

When a transaction involving self-dealing by a controlling shareholder is challenged, the applicable standard of judicial review is entire fairness, with the defendants having the burden of persuasion.[6] Judicial review for entire fairness of how the transaction was structured, negotiated, disclosed to the directors, and approved by the directors will be significantly influenced by evidence relating to the functioning of the special committee and the disinterestedness and independence of its members.

When determining whether a financial interest, personal relationship, or other alleged conflict compromises the disinterestedness and independence of an outside director, the court must determine whether the alleged conflict is material. The simple fact that the director has some financial ties or personal relationships is not sufficient. The Delaware Supreme Court has repeatedly held that any board process is materially enhanced when the decision is attributable to independent directors.

- Burden of the proof

The defendants bear the burden of proving that the transaction with the controlling stockholder was entirely fair to the minority stockholders. The defendants may seek to lower the standard of review from entire fairness by showing that the controller did not stand on both sides of the transaction. One means of accomplishing this is by using procedural devices such as (i) the creation of a sufficiently authorized board committee composed of independent and disinterested directors or (ii) the conditioning of the transaction on the affirmative vote of a majority of the shares owned by stockholders who are not affiliated with the controller.

In Weinberger,[7] the Delaware Supreme Court held that the entire fairness standard requires compliance with the duty of disclosure and incorporated this principle into the fair dealing aspect of the test. When conducting a fair price inquiry as part of the entire fairness standard of review, the court asks whether the transaction was one that a reasonable seller, under all of the circumstances, would regard as within a range of fair value; one that such a seller could reasonably accept. A price may fall within the range of fairness for purposes of the entire fairness test even though the point calculation demanded by the appraisal statute yields an award in excess of the merger price.

- Remedies in Entire Fairness

Three fundamental remedies: (i) rescission; (ii) rescissory damages; and (iii) quasi appraisal.

(i) Rescissory damages

Rescissory damages—a money award designed to be as nearly as possible the financial equivalent of rescission, is another possibility where a substantial delay occurs between the merger and trial. Rescissory damages are the monetary equivalent of rescission and may be awarded where the equitable remedy of rescission is impractical. The remedy is available for an adjudicated breach of the duty of loyalty, such as cases involving self-dealing or where a fiduciary puts personal interests ahead of the interests of its beneficiary.[8] In a case where a disloyal fiduciary wrongfully deprives its beneficiary of property, the rescissory damages measure seeks (i) to restore the plaintiff-beneficiary to the position it could have been in had the plaintiff or a faithful fiduciary exercised control over the property in the interim and (ii) to force the defendant to disgorge profits that the defendant may have achieved through the wrongful retention of the plaintiff's property. In a case involving corporate stock, rescissory damages can be measured at the time of judgment, the time of resale or at an intervening point when the stock had a higher value and remained in control of the disloyal fiduciary.[9] An award of rescissory damages is one form of relief that could be imposed if the merger is found not to be entirely fair and if one or more of the defendants are found to have violated their fiduciary duty of loyalty. Any award of rescissory damages only would be imposed on those fiduciaries who committed a loyalty breach.

(ii) Quasi appraisal

Quasi-appraisal is simply a shorthand description of a measure of damages. It refers to the quantum of money equivalent to what a stockholder would have received in an appraisal, namely the fair value of the stockholder's proportionate share of the equity of the corporation as a going concern. This measure is a form of compensatory or out-of-pocket damages, which are generally measured by the harm inflicted on the plaintiff at the time of the wrong. Quasi-appraisal contrasts with other potential measures of damages, such as reliance damages, expectancy damages, rescissory damages, disgorgement, and punitive damages. Because quasi-appraisal is a measure of damages, different causes of action can give rise to a quasi-appraisal remedy, just as different causes of action can give rise to other forms of remedies. The premise for the award is that without the disclosure of false or misleading information, or the failure to disclose material information, stockholders could have voted down the transaction and retained their proportionate share of the equity in the corporation as a going concern. Quasi-appraisal damages serve as a monetary substitute for the proportionate share of the equity that the stockholders otherwise would have retained.

(iii) Rescission

In a traditional rescission, all the transactions are called off. For instance, the minority shareholders challenging a merger would normally be entitled to have the merger rescinded and their former shares returned to them.

7.4 Staggered Boards

The staggered board, also known as "a classified board," is a mechanism, which allows a board of directors to be elected to staggered terms, typically over three years, rather than annually.[10] When a board of directors is staggered, only one-third of the directors are up for re-election in any given year. Staggered board are formidable antitakeover protection. Staggered boards are controversial because they enable directors to resist shareholder attempts to change control of the firm. As directors on a typical staggered board serve a term of approximately three years, a staggered board structure gives incumbent directors substantial protection from removal or attempts to gain control via either a proxy fight or a takeover bid.[11] Thus, the number of Standard & Poor 500 (S&P 500) companies with staggered boards has declined by 80%, from 300 in the year 2000 to 60 in 2013. As of January 2017, less than 105 of the corporations in the S&P 500 have staggered boards[12] In 2020, almost half of Russell 3000 companies continue to use some form of plurality voting to elect their directors and to retain classified board structures where directors do not face annual elections.[13]

7.4.1 Pros

Proponents of staggered board claim that a staggered board helps firms maintain stability, continuity, and independence within the board and enables management to pursue long-term strategic plans. That is, absent a staggered board such plans could be frustrated by a hostile offer or could make management forgo value-increasing long-term projects that appear unprofitable in the short-term. More, advocates of staggered boards allege that the insulation from shareholder intervention is beneficial as it gives directors significant time to learn the business they have been entrusted and to make better investment and operating decisions. Thus, directors would have enough time to focus on the long-run business purpose. A staggered board of directors facing takeover bid can better resist, push back, and protect the interests of the shareholders. Staggered boards are associated with lower firm valuations, as measured by Tobin's Q.[14] Furthermore, staggered-board firms tend to make value-decreasing acquisitions. Supporters of staggered boards argue that they can encourage innovation or investment, particularly at firms that require a long horizon to execute their strategy and whose outside investors are likely to be less informed about the firm's value. The insulation that staggered boards provide may be more beneficial to firms, subject to the pressures and earnings expectations of Wall Street analysts, which critics assert can lead to managerial myopia.

7.4.2 Cons

Conversely, opponents of staggered boards alleged that they harm shareholders by insulating directors and managers from the beneficial disciplinary forces of shareholder control, or the takeover market principle Staggered boards decrease merger activity by protecting a company from an unsolicited takeover. In the market for corporate control, if a target company has a staggered board, the hostile bidder must sustain a proxy contest through at least two annual meeting cycles in order to obtain control of the target's board. Others have argued that staggered boards can lead to self-seeking for directors and managers who have failed to deliver up to the shareholders' expectations to block any acquisition attempt.

7.4.3 Case Law

The Delaware Court of Chancery and Delaware Supreme Court rulings of October 8, 2010 and November 23, 2010, respectively, in the takeover battle between Airgas Inc. and Air Products and Chemicals, Inc. The rulings focused on the permissibility of shareholder-adopted bylaw amendments that substantially weaken the antitakeover force of staggered boards, arising from Air Products' battle to take over Airgas. The Delaware Chancery Court initially ruled that such shareholder-adopted bylaw amendments are permissible, but the Delaware Supreme Court subsequently reversed and held such measures to be invalid.

Facts:

- On February 11, 2010, Air Products announced Airgas rejected an all-cash tender offer at that price for 100% of Airgas shares at $60 per share. Air Products continued to raise its bids over the next few months, each being met with cool rejection.
- On July 8, it increased its offer to $63.50 per share, and on September 6, it raised its bid to $65.50 per share.

- The Airgas board of directors determined that each offer undervalued the company. During this entire attempted takeover period, the market price of Airgas stock exceeded Air Products' offers.
- Because Airgas has a staggered board consisting of three classes, only one-third of its nine directors came up for reelection at the meeting. With a majority of Airgas's shareholders seemingly supportive of this acquisition attempt, Air Products was able to replace the directors up for reelection in the September 2010 shareholder meeting with three individuals whom it had nominated.
- At the September 2010 annual meeting, Air Products obtained majority shareholder approval for a new shareholder-adopted bylaw provision (the Airgas bylaw), which specified that the next annual meeting would be held on January 18, 2011, a mere four months after the September 2010 annual meeting.
- Airgas brought this action in the Court of Chancery, claiming that the January Bylaw is invalid because it is inconsistent with title 8, section 141 of the Delaware Code and the Airgas corporate charter provision that creates a staggered board. Airgas's charter requires an affirmative vote of the holders of at least 67% of the voting power of all shares to alter, amend, or repeal the staggered board provision, or to adopt any bylaw inconsistent with that provision.
- The Court of Chancery upheld the January Bylaw on the following basis: Airgas's charter provides that directors serve terms that expire at "the annual meeting of stockholders held in the third year following the year of their election." There is no inconsistency between Airgas's charter provision and the January Bylaw, because the January meeting would occur "in the third year after the directors' election," which (the Court of Chancery found) was all that the Airgas charter requires.
- Air Products argued that the charter provision establishing a staggered board should be interpreted as requiring only that one-third of the directors come up for election in each calendar year's annual meeting, without limiting the ability of bylaws to specify the time during the calendar year in which the annual meeting would take place.
- On October 8, 2010, the Delaware Court of Chancery (Chancellor William Chandler) issued an opinion that sided with Air Product and approved the legality of the Air gas by-law.

- Airgas appealed to the Supreme Court of Delaware, which held a hearing on the case on November 2.
- The Delaware Supreme Court looked to extrinsic evidence to interpret the intent of the charter language, which provided that directors' terms expire at "the annual meeting of stockholders held in the third year following the year of their election."
- The Supreme Court found that the language has been understood to mean that the Airgas directors serve three-year terms. Therefore, because the January Bylaw prematurely terminated the Airgas directors' terms, conferred by the charter and the statute, by eight months, the January Bylaw was invalid. Accordingly, the Supreme Court reversed the Chancery Court holding.

Legal Insights
Proxy fight

1. Schnell v. Chris-Craft Industries, Inc., Del. Supr., 285 A. 2d 437 (1971):

Management may not inequitably manipulate corporate machinery to perpetuate "itself in office" and, to that end, for the purpose of obstructing the legitimate efforts of dissident stockholders in the exercise of their rights to undertake a proxy contest against management. Moreover, stockholders may not be charged with the duty of anticipating inequitable action by management, and of seeking anticipatory injunctive relief to foreclose such action, simply because the new Delaware Corporation Law makes such inequitable action legally possible.
Facts:

- Some dissident shareholders of Chris-Craft Industries, Inc. wished to replace the existing directors at the next annual meeting, scheduled in the bylaws for January 11, 1972.
- The directors employed various tactics to make the contest more difficult for the dissidents. They refused to turn over their list of shareholders and hired proxy solicitors to work on their behalf.
- At the October 18, 1971 board meeting, the directors invoked a new provision of the Delaware Corporate Law to advance the date of the annual meeting by a month, to December 8, 1971. This change

made it virtually impossible for the dissident shareholders to wage a successful proxy contest to unseat the incumbent directors.

- The dissident shareholders petitioned the court to enjoin an injunctive relief to prevent management from advancing the date of the annual stockholders' meeting from January 11, 1972, as previously set by the by-laws, to December 8, 1971.
- The trial court denied the petition, and the shareholders appealed.
- The Delaware Supreme Court reversed and remanded, with instructions to nullify the December 8 date as a meeting date for stockholders; to reinstate January 11, 1972 as the sole date of the next annual meeting of the stockholders of the corporation; and to take such other proceedings and action as may be consistent herewith regarding the stock record closing date and any other related matters.

2. *Blasius Corp. v. Atlas Corp.*, 564 A.2d 651 (Del. Ch. 1988):

Any action, which has the "primary purpose" of impeding the exercise of the stockholder franchise required an enhanced judicial scrutiny, pursuant to which the board of directors "bears the heavy burden of demonstrating a compelling justification for such action." Moreover, good faith belief by the incumbent board of directors that the leveraged recapitalization proposed was ill advised and less valuable than the company's business plan, were not a proper basis for interfering with the stockholder franchise in a contested election for successor directors.
Facts:

- On October 29, Blasius Industries, Inc. filed a Schedule 13D with the Securities Exchange Commission disclosing that, with affiliates, it then owed 9.1% of Atlas' Corporation common stock.
- On December 2, 1997, Blasius suggested that Atlas engage in a leveraged restructuring and distribute cash to shareholders. In such a transaction, which was by this date a commonplace form of transaction, a corporation typically raises cash by sale of assets and significant borrowings and makes a large one-time cash distribution to shareholders.
- The directors of Atlas believed this was not in the company's best interest and rejected the idea.
- On December 30, 1987, Blasius formalized their proposal and requested the election of eight new board members. This would increase the size of the board from eight to 15, the maximum allowed under the corporate charter.

- Fearing a takeover by Blasius, the board held an emergency meeting the next day and amended the bylaws to add two additional board members. The move was designed to prevent Blasius from seizing an eight to seven advantage on the board at the next election.
- Blasius filed suit that day in this court seeking a declaration that certain bylaws adopted by the board on September 1, 1987 acted as an unlawful restraint on the shareholders' right, created by Section 228 of our corporation statute, to act through consent without undergoing a meeting.
- The Atlas Corporation board convened a meeting, whereby the board voted to amend the bylaws to increase the size of the board from seven to nine and appointed John M. Devaney and Harry J. Winters, Jr. to fill those newly created positions.
- The Court found that while the addition of these qualified men would, under other circumstances, be clearly appropriate as an independent step, such a step was in fact taken in order to impede or preclude a majority of the shareholders from effectively adopting the course proposed by Blasius.
- The Atlas Corporation board resolution constituted an unintended violation of the duty of loyalty that the board owed to the shareholders.

3. *MM Co, Inc. v. Liquid Audio, Inc.*, 813 A.2d 1118, 1132 (Del. 2003):

The Delaware Supreme Court found that the primary purpose of the action was to diminish the influence of MM's nominees and that there was no compelling justification for the board's action.
Facts:

- For more than a year, MM sought to obtain control of Liquid Audio.
- On October 26, 2001, MM sent a letter to the Liquid Audio board of directors indicating its willingness to acquire the company at approximately $3 per share. Liquid Audio had a staggered board with five total members.
- Liquid Audio's board rejected MM's offer as inadequate, after an analysis of the offer and consultation with its investment banker, Broadview International LLC.
- On May 30, 2002, MM filed an action under Section 220 seeking, among other things, an order of the Court of Chancery directing that Liquid Audio forward to MM the information identified in the demand letter. A hearing before the Court of Chancery with respect

to the Section 220 complaint was scheduled to be held on June 14, 2002.

- In June 2002, MM launched a proxy campaign for the 2002 shareholders meeting. It nominated two candidates to fill the two board positions up for election that year, and also proposed to add four positions to the board and nominated candidates for those seats.
- If approved, MM's proposals would have granted it control of Liquid Audio's board.
- The shareholders' meeting was scheduled for September 26, 2002.
- By mid-August, it became clear that at a minimum, MM would be successful in electing its two candidates for the open board seats.
- On August 23, Liquid Audio's board announced that it had amended the bylaws to increase the size of the board to seven members, and that it had filled the new vacancies with two of its candidates.
- At the shareholders meeting, MM's two candidates were elected, but the shareholders rejected its proposal to expand the board by four members.
- MM sued Liquid Audio and its five directors, challenging the August 23 expansion of the board. MM argued that the expansion frustrated MM's efforts to obtain a substantial presence on the board, and that it improperly interfered with the shareholder franchise.
- In its amended complaint, MM argued that Liquid Audio's decision to expand the Board violated the principles established by Blasius and Unocal.
- The Court of Chancery ruled in favor of Liquid Audio, holding that the Board expansion did not violate Delaware law under either Blasius or Unocal. The Court of Chancery rejected MM independent Blasius' claim on the basis that the addition of two new directors "did not impact the shareholder vote or the shareholder choices in any significant way." The Court of Chancery rejected the MM Unocal claim, on the basis that: MM did "not contend that the board expansion was coercive," the expansion was not "preclusive," because the "choices that the shareholders had before the board action was taken were the same as they had after," and MM failed to make a showing that "the action that the board took falls outside a range of reasonable responses."
- After a trial, the Court of Chancery found that the board had acted with the primary purpose of diminishing the effectiveness of MM's two elected board members.

- The court also found, however, that the board expansion was a valid defensive measure under the *Unocal* test because it was reasonable in relation to the threat posed.
- MM appealed, raising two issues on appeal:
  - First, it contends that the Court of Chancery erred in ruling that the "compelling justification" standard, as enunciated in Blasius, was not applicable to the Board's action. In support of that argument, MM relied upon the finding by the Court of Chancery that Liquid Audio's Directors manipulated the size and composition of the Liquid Audio board during a contested election for directors primarily to interfere with and impede the success of MM's ability to gain two-of-five directorships on the Board, and, thus, to diminish the influence of MM's nominees on the Board.
  - Second, MM argued that the Court of Chancery erred in ruling that the precepts of this Court's holding in Unocal and its progeny were not violated by the Board's defensive action. According to MM, Liquid Audio Directors never identified a legally cognizable threat to the corporate policy and effectiveness of Liquid Audio and, to the extent that a threat existed, never demonstrated that the "manipulation of the size and composition" of the Liquid Audio board was a reasonable response in relation to such threat. Based upon that asserted lack of record evidence, MM submitted the Court of Chancery erred in concluding that this Court's holding in Unocal was not violated.
- The Delaware Supreme Court held that Since Liquid Audio Directors did not demonstrate a compelling justification for that defensive action, the bylaw amendment that expanded the size of the Liquid Audio board, and permitted the appointment of two new members on the eve of a contested election, should have been invalidated by the Court of Chancery.
- That the incumbent Board timed its utilization of these otherwise valid powers to expand the size and composition of the Liquid Audio board for the primary purpose of impeding and interfering with the efforts of the stockholders' power to effectively exercise their voting rights in a contested election for directors.

4. *San Antonio Fire & Police Pension Fund v. Amylin Pharmaceuticals., Inc.* 2009 (Del. Ch. May 12, 2009).

The *Amylin* litigation grew out of a proxy contest in which insurgents Eastbourne Capital Management, L.L.C. and Icahn Partners LP each nominated five directors for election to Amylin's 12-member board. The Court held that directors are while relying in good faith on the information available to them at the time, even if they were later proved wrong.

Facts:

- On June 8, 2007, Amylin Pharmaceuticals, Inc. issued a series of convertible senior notes due 2014.
- The Notes were governed by an indenture with The Bank of New York Mellon Trust Company, N.A. as the trustee.
- The Indenture contained restrictions on a change of control (the "Continuing Directors Provision"), which gave noteholders the right to require Amylin to repurchase any or all of their notes at face value, upon the occurrence of a Fundamental Change, which is defined to occur, among other times, when "at any time the Continuing Directors do not constitute a majority of the Company's Board of Directors."
- On January 28, 2009, Icahn Partners LP and affiliates notified Amylin of its intention to nominate a slate of five directors to Amylin's 12-member board.
- On January 29, 2009, Eastbourne Capital Management, L.L.C. notified Amylin of its intention to nominate its own five-person slate.
- On March 9, 2009, Eastbourne sent a letter to the Board urging it to "approve" the dissident slates for purposes of the Indenture.
- The indenture defined the term "Continuing Directors" to include the individuals constituting Amylin's board on the date the notes were issued, as well as any new directors whose election to Amylin's board, or whose nomination for election, "was approved by at least a majority of the directors then still in office either who were directors on the issuance or whose election or nomination for election was previously so approved."
- On March 24, 2009, San Antonio Fire & Police Pension Fund filed a class action complaint against Amylin and each of its directors alleging:

    i. breaches of the fiduciary duties of care and loyalty by the Board in the adoption of the Indenture and a certain credit agreement,

ii. breaches of the fiduciary duties of care and loyalty in failing to approve the dissident nominees in order to defuse the Continuing Directors Provision, and
iii. breaches of the fiduciary duties of care and loyalty in the allegedly misleading and coercive manner in which the Board disclosed the risks presented by the continuing directors provisions in the company's Form 10-K.

- Amylin's board "approved" the insurgent nominees as "Continuing Directors" for purposes of the indenture, while continuing to oppose the insurgents and to recommend its own slate for purposes of the proxy contest.
- Prior to approving the dissident nominees, Amylin sought confirmation of its view from the Trustee, and the Trustee declined to provide the confirmation requested.
- Amylin filed a cross-claim against the Trustee, and sought declaratory relief that the Board had the right under the Indenture to approve the election of any or all of the stockholder nominees while simultaneously recommending against their election to the Board. The Fund also amended its complaint to add the Trustee as a necessary defendant, seeking a declaration that the Board has the sole right and power to approve the stockholder nominees for purposes of the Continuing Directors Provision.
- On May 4, 2009, Eastbourne filed its definitive proxy statement, in which it reduced the number of candidates it was nominating to the Board from five to three.
- On May 6, 2009, Icahn filed its definitive proxy statement in which it reduced the number of candidates it was nominating to the Board from five to two.
- The reduction in the total number of dissident directors eliminated the possibility that at the upcoming election a majority of the Board will cease to be Continuing Directors.
- The Court held that the Board was authorized to approve the stockholder-nominated directors, and thereby avoid triggering the Put Option, as long as such approval was given in good faith and in accordance with the Board's fiduciary duties.
- The Court's ruling that the Board has the power under the terms of the Indenture to approve the stockholder nominees was based on the contractual interpretation of the Continuing Directors Provision and the meaning of the word "approve."

- The Court also rejected the San Antonio Fire & Police Pension Fund claim that the Board breached its duty of care when it adopted the Indenture because it had failed to learn of the existence of the Continuing Directors Provision.
- The Court found that the duty of care did not require the Board to review and consider every term of the Indenture. The Court noted that change of control provisions in debt instruments can function as possible entrenchment devices that coerce stockholders into voting only for directors nominated by a company's incumbent board, and raise concerns related to whether boards of directors violate fiduciary duties in agreeing to provisions that may eviscerate the stockholder franchise.

Notes

1. Financier Worldwide (2015): *The Importance of Corporate Social Responsibility.*
2. Jian Huang and Gokhan Torna (2017): How Proxy Contests Affect Corporate Policy, Columbia Law School's Blog on Corporations and thee Capital Markets.
3. Malone v. Brincat, 722 A.2d 5, 12 (Del. 1998).
4. TSC Indus., Inc. v. Northway, Inc., 426 U.S. 438, 449 (1976).
5. In re Dollar Thrifty Shareholder Litigation, 14 A.3d 573, 598 (Del. Ch. 2010).
6. Ams. Mining Corp. v. Theriault, 51 A.3d 1213, 1239 (Del. 2012).
7. Weinberger v. UOP, Inc., 457 A.2d 701, 710 (Del. 1983).
8. Strassburger v. Earley, 752 A.2d 557, 581 (Del. Ch. 2000).
9. Duncan v. TheraTx, Inc., 775 A.2d 1019, 1023 (Del. 2000).
10. Yakov Amihud, Markus Schmid, & Steven D. Solomon (2018): Settling the Staggered Board, University of Pennsylvania Law Review, Volume 166:1475, p. 1480.
11. Alma Cohen (2013): How Do Staggered Boards Affect Shareholder Value? Evidence from a Natural Experiment, Journal of Financial Economics, p. 6.
12. Zohar Goshen, Sharon Hannes (2018): The Death of Corporate law, ECGI, Law Working Paper No. 402/2018, p. 14.

13. Matteo Tonello (2020): Corporate Board Practices in the Russell 3000 and S&P 500, HLS Corporate Governance Forum.
14. Robert Daines (2016): Can Staggered Boards Improve Value? Evidence from the Massachusetts Natural Experiment, *Stanford Law School*.

CHAPTER 8

Shareholders Appraisal Rights and Valuation

8.1 General

Valuation and/or appraisal aims to determine the fair value of a company. *The concept of fair value under Delaware law is not equivalent to the economic concept of fair market value. Rather, the concept of fair value for purposes of Delaware's appraisal statute is a largely judge-made creation, freighted with policy considerations. That is,* fair value is a law-created valuation method that excludes elements of value that would normally be captured in economic models. In using "all relevant factors" to determine fair value, the Court has significant discretion to use the valuation methods it deems appropriate, including the parties' proposed valuation frameworks, or one of the Court's own making. More, courts relied on multiple valuation techniques to determine fair value, giving greater weight to the more reliable methodologies in a comparable case. Under Del Code § 262(h), *Courts must determine the fair value of the shares exclusive of any element of value arising from the accomplishment or expectation of the merger or consolidation.* Courts assess the fair value of each share of stock "on the closing date of the merger" and determine the value of the pre-merger corporation as a going concern. Courts also rely upon valuation experts' determination. The valuation analyst's fairness opinion typically consists of a written opinion and may be accompanied by a financial analysis that includes a range of value. Valuation analysts may

F. Lessambo, *U.S. Mergers and Acquisitions*,
https://doi.org/10.1007/978-3-030-85735-6_8

be retained to provide fairness opinions for private company M&A transactions. Many private companies conduct the transaction with in-house staff, or a private equity firm that has M&A expertise may own them.

8.2 Shareholders Appraisal Rights

An appraisal proceeding is a limited legislative remedy intended to provide shareholders dissenting from a merger on grounds of inadequacy of the offering price with a judicial determination of the intrinsic worth (fair value) of their shareholdings.[2] Through such proceeding, the Court shall determine the fair value of the shares exclusive of any element of value arising from the accomplishment or expectation of the merger or consolidation, together with interest, if any, to be paid upon the amount determined to be the fair value.

Prior to its 2007 amendments, that Section provided in part:

> After determining the stockholders entitled to an appraisal, the Court shall appraise the shares, determining their fair value exclusive of any element of value arising from the accomplishment or expectation of the merger or consolidation, together with a fair rate of interest, if any, to be paid upon the amount determined to be the fair value. In determining the fair rate of interest, the Court may consider all relevant factors, including the rate of interest, which the surviving or resulting corporation would have had to pay to borrow money during the pendency of the proceeding.[3]

In 2007, the General Assembly revised its views on interest, and Section 262(h) now provides, in part:

> Unless the Court in its discretion determines otherwise for good cause shown, interest from the effective date of the merger through the date of payment of the judgment shall be compounded quarterly and shall accrue at 5% over the Federal Reserve discount rate (including any surcharge) as established from time to time during the period between the effective date of the merger and the date of payment of the judgment.

Under Section 262 of the Delaware General Corporation Law, stockholders who meet certain requirements are entitled to an appraisal by the Court of Chancery of the fair value of their shares of stock.[4] An appraisal must be focused on [respondent's] going concern value. The appraisal right was intended to protect—stockholders—who due to the statute lost their common law right to prevent a merger—by providing for the appraisement of their stock and the payment to them of the full value thereof in money.

Consistent with Section 262, Delaware courts routinely and properly exclude elements of value arising from a merger or the expectation of a merger in appraisal proceedings. For example, Delaware courts exclude considerations that would result from synergies following a merger and look to the company's unaffected, pre-merger announcement stock price to determine its fair value or fair price—much like how ACLI's expert looked to the yield-to-worst cost of the Notes immediately prior to the Merger Announcement Date rather than when it was affected by the Merger Announcement.

During such an appraisal proceeding, the Court of Chancery shall determine the fair value of the shares exclusive of any element of value arising from the accomplishment or expectation of the merger or consolidation, together with interest, if any, to be paid upon the amount determined to be the fair value. In determining such fair value, the Court shall take into account all relevant factors:

- Market value,
- Asset value,
- Dividends,
- Earning prospects,
- The nature of the enterprise, and
- any other facts which were known or which could be ascertained as of the date of merger and which throw any light on future prospects of the merged corporation are not only pertinent to an inquiry as to the value of the dissenting stockholders' interest, but must be considered by the agency fixing the value.

In an appraisal proceeding, both sides have the burden of proving their respective valuations by a preponderance of the evidence.[5]

8.3 Valuation Techniques

8.3.1 Discounted Cash Flow

- Concept of DCF

The Delaware Supreme Court previously found that DCF analysis was the best tool for appraising a company when market-based evidence was unavailable. This analysis requires three inputs: a projection of future cash flows, a terminal value, and a discount rate. The company's available cash is then added to this calculation, and its debt subtracted to arrive at a final enterprise value. The discounted cash flow model is only as reliable as the financial projections used in it and its other underlying assumptions. However, the DCF model has much less utility in cases where the transaction giving rise to appraisal was an arm's-length merger, [or] where the data used in the model are not reliable. In determining the cost of capital to be applied in DCF valuations, the Delaware Court of Chancery has primarily used the Capital Asset Pricing Model.

i. Free cash flows can be thought of as the cash generated by a company's net operating assets before any payments are made to debtholders in the form of interest and/or principal to shareholders in the form of dividends. They include several inputs, including: Earnings Before Interest, Taxes, Depreciation, and Amortization ("EBITDA"); capital expenditures ("CAPEX")—the money a company spends on maintaining and upgrading its capital stock—and changes in working capital and taxes.

ii. Discount rate

Discount rates are the second crucial ingredient of a DCF analysis. Discount rates reflect the commonsense notion that a dollar tomorrow is not as valuable as a dollar today. Accordingly, a discount rate is applied to each future cash flow to determine that cash flow's present value. The applied discount rate reflects a combination of factors and can be calculated in several different ways. In general, experts rely on the well-accepted weighted average cost of capital ("WACC") methodology in calculating discount rate. WACC is the "cost of capital (discount rate)" determined by the weighted average, at market value, of the cost of all financing sources in the business enterprise's capital structure. The WACC is based on the debt/equity ratio in the company's actual or intended capital structure at the valuation date, not a hypothetical capital structure. When shares of the company being appraised were actively traded prior to the transaction, customary practice is to determine beta by reference to the company's market prices (e.g., Bloomberg betas). However, betas based on comparable companies are sometimes accepted, even in cases where the comparable company method has been rejected. The Court generally prefers betas based on longer periods, generally five years, but a two-year period is sometimes accepted.

iii. Terminal value

In a DCF analysis, future cash flows are only projected out for a certain period of time (i.e., 5, 10, and 15 years). Rather than continuing to forecast annual cash flows after this period, valuation experts typically calculate a firm's terminal value as an estimation of its cash flows into perpetuity. Two common methods for computing a firm's terminal value are (a) the perpetual growth model (commonly referred to as the Gordon Growth model) and (b) an exit multiples method (which assumes a sale of the company). The Delaware courts predominantly use a growth model to calculate terminal value. Nonetheless, multiples have been used only in cases where neither side's expert used a growth model. This terminal value is then discounted to a present value. As a company's terminal value can account for a large percentage of its value in a DCF, understanding the experts' disagreements on this point is essential.

- Court Cases:

1. In William Richard Kruse v. Synapse Wireless, Inc.[6]
    - The Delaware Court of Chancery held that, after its review of the evidence as fact finder, the Company had carried its burden of proving a reliable appraisal of its fair value related to its 2016 merger transaction.
    - In two rounds of investments, McWane Inc. (i) acquired a controlling interest in 2012, and, in 2016, the remaining Synapse shares in 2016 in a cash-out merger at $0.43 per share, but Kruse refused McWane's offer and filed this appraisal action in the Court of Chancery.

- At trial, Kruse's expert valued Synapse at $4.19 per share as of 2016, while Synapse's expert calculated a value between $0.06 and $0.11 per share. Both experts used three valuation methods: (i) a Prior Company Transaction analysis; (ii) a Comparable Transaction Analysis; and (iii) a Discounted Cash Flow (DCF) analysis.
- The Court of Chancery eschewed the first two valuation methods as unreliable, but adopted Synapse's DCF analysis with minor adjustments. The Court held that neither party had carried its burden to show that its Comparable Transaction Analysis reflected Synapse's fair value, as experts from each side raised thoughtful objections to the other's analyses, including the comparability of the transactions, and neither expert successfully rebutted the other's objections.
- The Court adopted the Company's discounted cash flow valuation method, eschewing all other methods as unreliable in this case. The Court's value was almost half of the merger transaction value upon which the stockholder exercised its appraisal rights.

2. *Hoyd v. Trussway Holdings LLC*, 2019 WL 994048[7] (Del Ch. Feb. 28, 2019)

- In February 2019, a shareholder who was squeezed out of Trussway, a private company, was awarded an amount 5% higher than the merger value.
- The Delaware Court of Chancery found DCF analysis was the best way to achieve fair value in a statutory appraisal arising out of a contested merger. The court's analysis relied heavily on company expert's analysis regarding contested inputs, including projections, beta, and terminal value.
- The Court averaged DCF calculations based on two periods: a nine-year management projection and the first five years of that projection. It described the five-year period as "more standard." The valuation based on the five-year period was 15% lower than the valuation based on the nine-year period.
- The Court *blended two DCF values, one derived from the nine-year Project Point Projections and a second derived from the same*

management forecasts, with a terminal period beginning after a more standard five years, and assigned 50% weight to each.

- Using the five-year period, the Court effectively substituted the 2.3% perpetual growth rate for the higher growth rate that management expected in the final four years.
- The Court agreed with the experts' view that an adjustment was necessary to a value based on the nine-year projection, and it explained its decision to give partial weight to the shorter period.

Of more concern to me is Trussway management's ability (or that of any human prognosticator) to accurately predict corporate performance nine years out, particularly concerning new facets of a business. I am also aware that there is a degree of huckster's optimism in these predictions.

3. *In re PLX Technology Inc. Shareholders Litigation.*, 2018 WL 5018353 (Del. Ch. Oct. 16, 2018)
   - *In re PLX Technology Inc. Shareholders Litigation.*, Vice Chancellor Laster found that the board's failure to disclose Deutsche Bank's "tip" to Singer in the Schedule 14D-9 was a material omission that amounted to a breach of the directors' duty of disclosure, and that Potomac had aided and abetted such breach through Singer's (its agent's) actions.

The key facts can be summarized as follows:

- PLX Technology Inc. was a publicly traded company that developed and sold specialized integrated circuits used in connectivity applications.
- In February 2013, Avago Technologies Wireless Manufacturing Inc. expressed interest in acquiring PLX for $6 per share.
- PLX's board told Avago that its offer would need to be at least $7 per share in order for PLX to consider it. Avago declined to raise its bid.
- Then after, Potomac Capital Partners II, L.P., an activist investor, acquired a stake in PLX for the express purpose of inducing PLX to sell itself to Avago.

- Following its investment in PLX, Potomac initiated a proxy contest, ultimately succeeding in installing its co-managing member, Singer, and two other nominees on PLX's board.
- While sitting on the board, Singer learned from Deutsche Bank (PLX's financial advisor) that it had been informed by Avago that once Avago completed a separate acquisition, it would be open to a potential acquisition of PLX for $300 million, equivalent to approximately $6.53 per share.
- Deutsche Bank was at that time also advising Avago on its other pending acquisition.
- Singer did not report this "tip" to the other members of the PLX board, but was later appointed chair of a Special Committee formed by the PLX board to run an affirmative process to consider the sale of the Company, a position, which would effectively allow him to run the sale process with Avago.
- Several months later, after closing its separate transaction, Avago submitted a proposal to acquire PLX at a price of $6.25 per share, which PLX countered at $6.75 per share.
- Just nine days later, PLX agreed in principle to Avago's "best and final proposal" of $6.50 per share, almost the exact amount Singer and Deutsche Bank had been told months earlier Avago was then prepared to pay (and notwithstanding the PLX board's previous refusal to entertain an offer from Avago under $7 per share).
- Vice Chancellor Laster concluded that plaintiffs, which legal theory was that the company should not have been sold at all—not that there was an alternative transaction at a higher price reasonably available—the measure of damages was the difference, if any, between the merger consideration and the company's "fair" or "intrinsic" value (which the court described as a "quasi-appraisal" remedy).
- That because PLX's sale was negotiated in an arm's-length transaction involving multiple potential bidders, the deal price must be afforded "heavy, if not overriding, probative value."
- Vice Chancellor Laster determined that the projections used by the plaintiffs' expert in his DCF calculations were flawed in three respects: (i) "the projections included a new line of business involving a new set of customers with a new set of requirements and evidence at trial did not give [the Court] sufficient confidence to base a damages award on this element of the projections"; (ii) "PLX management had a track record of missing its projections";

(iii) "bidders do not appear... to have believed that [the projection] supported valuations in the range that [plaintiffs' expert] posited.... If the projections were sufficiently reliable to support a credible valuation of $9.82 per share, then it seems likely that another buyer would have competed."

- The Supreme Court of Delaware affirmed the trial court's decision on the basis that although flawed from a fiduciary standpoint, the details of the sale process that the Board conducted and the nature of the synergistic deal with Avago that it generated mean that the plaintiffs received consideration that exceeded the value of the Company on a stand-alone basis.

8.3.2 Comparable Companies

- Concept

Comparable company method is accepted in the limited number of cases in which the court is satisfied as to comparability of selected companies. Comparable transactions are occasionally accepted but should be adjusted to eliminate synergies and other benefits. Comparable company's analysis provides relevant insights into the company's value based on inferences from how the market value[s] companies in the same industry, facing most of the same risks. However, the financial ratios utilized in "comparables" analyses can vary widely even within the same industry. Put differently, this method consists of comparing one business to publicly held firms whose stock is trading. The fair value is derived by examining the public firm's EV/EBITDA or EV/Revenue multiples and applying a similar multiple to the non-public, target firm.

(EV = Enterprise Value and EBITDA
= Earnings Before Interest Taxes, Depreciation, and Amortization).

As of January 2020, the average EV/EBITDA for the S&P 500 was 14.20. As a general guideline, an EV/EBITDA value below 10 is commonly interpreted as healthy and above average by analysts and investors. Put differently, to calculate enterprise value, determine the company's market capitalization by multiplying the company's outstanding shares by the current market price of one share. To this number, add the company's total long-term and short-term debt. Lastly, subtract the company's cash and cash equivalents.

- Court Case
- *In re Appraisal of DFC Global Corp.*[8]

The Supreme Court of Delaware reversed the Chancellor Court and endorsed the use of the comparable company method that had been used and accepted by both experts. Vice Chancellor Laster valued Dell at 27% above the deal price, solely using DCF, and gave no weight to the deal price for a series of reasons: (i) The market for Dell's shares was inefficient, and a valuation gap existed between market perception and Dell's operative reality, driven by analysts' focus on short-term results; (ii) deal prices in management buyout (MBO) transactions are unreliable as measures of fair value; (iii) the price that leveraged buyout (LBO) sponsors would pay is limited by the need to achieve IRRs of 20%+, and by limits on financial leverage; (iv) the shopping process was inadequate; and (v) financial sponsors are concerned about a "winner's curse."

The Supreme Court disagreed with each of the trial court's reasons for rejecting the deal price and relied upon the following: (i) The market for Dell's shares was efficient and there was no "valuation gap"; (ii) the transaction was not a management buyout; (iii) LBO sponsors' IRR requirements did not justify rejecting their bids as a measure of fair value; (iv) the shopping process was satisfactory; and (v) the Special Committee addressed the information asymmetry problem and the "winner's curse" risk as best it could. Therefore, the Supreme Court of Delaware concluded that:

> *Overall, the weight of evidence shows that Dell's deal price has heavy, if not overriding, probative value. ... [T]o the extent that the Court of Chancery chose to disregard Dell's deal price based on the presence of only private equity bidders, its reasoning is not grounded in accepted financial principles, and this assessment weighs in favor of finding an overall abuse of discretion.*

Discounted Cash Flow Analysis
(in millions)

	Fiscal Year Ending June 30					
	2014P	2015P	2016P	2017P	2018P	Terminal
EBITDA[1]	$143.3	$165.4	$214.9	$269.5	$329.4	
Less: Depreciation and Amortization	(44.8)	(45.1)	(46.4)	(46.6)	(46.6)	
Plus: Adjustment for SBC Accounting/Cash Difference[2]		5.6	6.4	6.8	7.0	
EBIT	$98.5	$125.9	$174.9	$229.7	$289.8	
Tax Rate		42.3%	35.9%	32.1%	30.7%	
Less: Income Tax		(53.3)	(62.8)	(73.7)	(89.0)	
Unlevered Net Income		**$72.7**	**$112.1**	**$156.0**	**$200.8**	
Plus: Depreciation & Amortization		45.1	46.4	46.6	46.6	
Less: Capital Expenditures		(35.8)	(42.6)	(44.1)	(45.7)	
Less: Changes in Working Capital[3]		(48.8)	(54.5)	(69.8)	(71.6)	
Unlevered Free Cash Flow[4]	**$2.1**	**$33.2**	**$61.4**	**$88.7**	**$130.1**	**$ 1,761**
Present Value of Distributable Cash Flows						
WACC	10.72%	10.72%	10.72%	10.72%	10.72%	10.72%
Discount Period (mid-year convention)	0.02	0.55	1.55	2.55	3.55	3.55
Present Value Factor	1.00	0.95	0.85	0.77	0.70	0.70
Present Value of Distributable Cash Flows	**$2.1**	**$31.4**	**$52.4**	**$68.4**	**$90.7**	**$1,226.6**

Enterprise Value

PV of Distributable Cash Flows (2014-2018)	$244.9
PV of Residual Cash Flows	$1,226.6
Cash and Equivalents	$51.5
Enterprise Value	**$1,523.0**
Add: PV of Net Operating Loss Balance[5]	$38.1
Less: Debt	$1,044.4
Equity Value	$516.74
Shares Outstanding[6]	39.53
Value Per Share	$13.07

Discount Rate	10.72%
Perpetuity Growth Rate	3.10%
Valuation Date	13-Jun-14

[1] Based on Beaulne's adjusted EBITDA, which includes full accounting SBC expense. Financial projections use Beaulne's model.
[2] Adds back difference between full accounting SBC expense and Dages' estimated SBC cash expense.
[3] Uses Beaulne's model but removes his adjustments to working capital based on 52.0% fixed rate assumption.
[4] 2014 unlevered cash flow based on Dages' calculation of prorated cash flow from June 13 until June 30.
[5] Based on Beaulne's NOL model, adjusted for 10.72% discount rate.
[6] Approximates adjusted shares outstanding using Dages' model and a $13 exercise price.

WACC Calculation

Peer Group Company	5Y Smoothed Bloomberg Beta	Total Debt ($000's)	Market Val of Equity ($000's)	Equity/Capital Ratio	Debt/Capital Ratio	Effective Tax Rate	Hamada Unlevered Beta
Cash America International, Inc.	0.9765	630,256	1,224,887	66.03%	33.97%	35.00%	0.7317
Cash Converters International Limited	0.8909	104,513	431,082	80.49%	19.51%	30.00%	0.7616
EZCORP, Inc.	1.1050	229,121	668,900	74.49%	25.51%	35.00%	0.9038
First Cash Financial Services Inc.	0.8951	200,000	1,551,881	88.58%	11.42%	35.00%	0.8259
International Personal Finance Plc	1.8789	664,292	2,435,081	78.57%	21.43%	21.00%	1.5458
World Acceptance Corp.	0.9972	505,500	761,218	60.09%	39.91%	38.25%	0.7072
DFC Global Corp.	1.1833			26.00%	74.00%	32.00%	0.4031

Peer Group & DFC Average Unlevered Beta:	0.8399
DFC Relevered Beta:	2.4653
Hamada Unlevered Beta = (Levered Beta) / (1 + (1-T)(Wd/We))	
Hamada Relevered Beta = Unlevered Beta * (1+(1-T)(Wd/We))	

Input	Value	Notes
Risk-free Rate (Rf)	3.14%	20-year Total Constant Maturity Treasury Yield
Beta (β)	2.4653	Avg. of 6 peers and DFC, relevered for DFC
Equity Risk Premium (ERP)	6.18%	Duff & Phelps Supply-Side Equity Risk Premium
Size Premium (SP)	3.52%	Duff & Phelps Size Premium, Subdecile 10w
Tax Rate (T)	32.00%	Management Assumption
Debt/Capital (Wd)	74.00%	Capital structure at close
Equity/Capital (We)	26.00%	Capital structure at close
Cost of Equity (Ke)	21.90%	Ke = Rf + (β * ERP) + SP
Cost of Debt (Kd)	10.00%	2016 Senior Note YTM
WACC	10.72%	WACC = (We * Ke) + (Wd * (Kd * (1 − T)))

8.3.3 Comparable Transactions

- Concept

Comparable transactions uses previously completed mergers and acquisitions deals involving similar companies to value a business. Comparable Transaction Analysis uses the same comparables described under the Comparable Companies' Analysis: Enterprise Value/Sales, Enterprise Value/EBITDA, and Earnings/Earnings Per Share (EPS) are the most commonly used metrics. However, unlike in Comparable Companies Analysis, the basis for value comparison is the ***price paid by the purchaser*** for a business, rather than the ***traded market values*** of the company's securities. The ideal comparable transaction is for a company in the same industry with a similar business model. The fair value of the takeover target is based on its recent earnings. More, Comparable Transaction Analysis tends to focus on the value of a business *as of the time an acquisition of the business can be completed, rather than today*. This is because deals take time to close, whereas current market values for a business can be assessed on any day. Below you will find a detailed overview of Precedent Transactions techniques used by investment bankers and leveraged buyout investors (also known as "financial sponsors") to value a company.

8.3.4 Asset Value

- Concept

An asset-based approach is a type of business valuation that focuses on a company's net asset value. The net asset value is identified by subtracting total liabilities from total assets. There is some room for interpretation in terms of deciding which of the company's assets and liabilities to include in the valuation and how to measure the worth of each. The assets being valued are both tangible and intangible which means they are considered in the valuation regardless of whether or not they show up on the balance sheet. The final value of the business is determined by a simple formula: Assets – Liabilities = Value of the Business.

8.3.5 *Transaction Price*

- Concept

The transaction price provides fair value when it is the product of an arm's-length process and a robust bidding environment; the transaction price method is reliable only when the market conditions leading to the transaction are conducive to achieving a fair price. The advantage of an arm's-length transaction price as a reliable indicator of fair value is that it is "forged in the crucible of objective market reality" (as distinguished from the unavoidably subjective thought process of a valuation expert).

- Court cases

In re Appraisal of Columbia Pipeline Group, Inc.,[9] 2019 WL 3778370 (Del. Ch. Aug. 12, 2019).

- *In re Appraisal of Columbia Pipeline Group,* the court found that the deal process was characterized by objective indicia of reliability sufficient to make the deal price the most reliable metric of fair value.
- The Vice Chancellor Laster rejected petitioners' claim that the DCF and the unaffected market price were the most appropriate methods based upon facts and circumstances, and that the company's value increased between signing and closing.
- Petitioners' DCF valuation was 24% over the deal price and 57% over unaffected market.
- VC Laster rejected their DCF analysis as contrary to contemporaneous market evidence:

[Expert]'s opinion that the value of Columbia materially exceeded the deal price conflicts with the market behavior of other potential strategic acquirers who had shown interest in Columbia, and who did not step forward to top TransCanada's price.

Rather, VC Laster observed that the wide swings in output that result from legitimate debate over reasonable inputs undermine the reliability of [petitioner's expert]'s DCF model.

8.3.6 Unaffected Market Price

- Concept

Though the appraisal statute empowers the Court to consider "all relevant factors" in determining fair value, the Delaware Supreme Court has clarified the particular importance of certain market-based factors, namely unaffected market price and merger consideration. The unaffected market price comprises "the collective judgment of the many based on all the publicly available information about a given company and the value of its shares." It is an "important indicator" of fair value (so long as the stock is trading in an efficient market) deal price that is the product of "a robust market check will often be the most reliable evidence of fair value."

- Court case

(Case 1) in Re Appraisal of Jarden Corp.[10]

- *In re Appraisal of Jarden Corp.*, Vice Chancellor Joseph R. Slights held that the unaffected market price was the best indicator of the fair value of Jarden's stock (representing a 18.4% discount to the merger consideration).
- The Court first found that the market for Jarden's stock was efficient based on testimony by the company's expert, who looked at factors such as Jarden's market capitalization, trading volume, bid-ask spread, number of analysts, and event studies.
- The Vice Chancellor found that the deal price, though relevant, was less reliable than the unaffected market price due to the flawed sale process undertaken by the Jarden Board of Directors.
- The Court rejected the petitioners' argument that the unaffected market price was unreliable because the market was unaware of material facts about Jarden's stand-alone prospects.
- Likewise, the Court found that the deal price was unreliable due to a flawed sale process.
- Rather, *Vice Chancellor* Joseph noted that (i) Jarden had no control shareholders, (ii) 94% of its shares were in the public float, (ii) the bid-ask spread was only 0.02%, and (iv) approximately 20 analysts had published reports on Jarden in the year prior to the merger.

(Case 2): In Re Appraisal of Stillwater Mining Co.[11]

- In re Appraisal of Stillwater Mining Co., Vice Chancellor Laster determined that the deal price was the best indicator of the fair value of a business in a major appraisal case, as neither side proved that its DCF valuation provided a persuasive indicator of fair value. The experts disagreed over too many inputs, and the resulting valuation swings were too great.
- In fact, Stillwater and Sibanye had negotiated an agreement and plan of merger dated December 9, 2016, pursuant to which each share of Stillwater common stock was converted to a right to receive $18.00.
- Petitioners in the matter argued that the sale process was insufficient and that Stillwater's fair value was $25.91 per share, which they supported with the opinion of an expert who utilized a discounted cash flow (DCF) model to value Stillwater.
- On the reverse, Sibanye argued that the fair value of Stillwater was $17.63 per share, a price the Buyer substantiated by relying upon the deal price, Stillwater's unaffected trading price, and an expert valuation that also relied upon a DCF model.
- The Court found that the deal price is the most persuasive indicator of fair value. Relying on any of the other valuation metrics would introduce error. The fair value of Stillwater on the valuation date was therefore $18.00 per share.

Valuation Methods Used in Delaware Appraisal Decisions

	Number of Valuations	*DCF or similar*	*Comparable Companies*	*Comparable Transactions*	*Asset Value*	*Transaction Price*	*Unaffected Mkt. Price*
	Arm's-Length Transactions						
1998–2005	2	2	0	0	0	1	0
2006–2013	4	3	1	0	0	2	0
2014–2019	14	6	2	1	0	12	2(a)
Total	20	11	3	1	0	15	2
	Related Party Transactions						
1998–2005	14	8	7	4	0	0	0

(continued)

(continued)

	Number of Valuations	*DCF or similar*	*Comparable Companies*	*Comparable Transactions*	*Asset Value*	*Transaction Price*	*Unaffected Mkt. Price*
2006–2013	7	7	1	1	1	0	0
2014–2019	9	9	0	0	0	0	0
Total	30	24	8	5	1	0	0

(a) One Court of Chancery decision using unaffected market price was reversed, and the other is being appealed

Source AICPA, Forensics & Valuation Services Conference (2019)

Notes

1. Samuel S. Nicholls (2020): The Role of the Investment Banker Compared to the Independent Valuation Analyst in M&A Transactions and Litigation.
2. Ala. By-Prods. Corp. v. Neal, 588 A.2d 255, 256 (Del. 1991).
3. 8 Del. C. § 262(h)(2001).
4. 8 Del. C. § 262.
5. M.G. Bancorporation, Inc. v. LeBeau, 737 A.2d 513, 520 (Del. 1999).
6. In William Richard Kruse v. Synapse Wireless, Inc., C.A. No. 12392-VCS (Del. Ch. July 14, 2020).
7. *Hoyd v. Trussway Holdings LLC*, 2019 WL 994048 (Del Ch. Feb. 28, 2019).
8. *In re Appraisal of DFC Global Corp.*, 2016 Del. Ch. LEXIS 103 (Del. Ch. July 8, 2016).
9. In re Appraisal of Columbia Pipeline Group, Inc., 2019 WL 3778370 (Del. Ch. Aug. 12, 2019).
10. *In re Appraisal of Jarden Corp.*, 2019 WL 3244085 (Del. Ch. July 19, 2019).
11. In re Appraisal of Stillwater Mining Co., 2019 WL 3943851 (Del. Ch. Aug. 21, 2019).

CHAPTER 9

Structuring Acquisitions

9.1 General

In order to prepare a definitive acquisition agreement, the parties need to determine the structure of the proposed transaction. Finding a proper deal structure is a critical component in promoting the feasibility of a merger or acquisition. Each structure contains advantages and disadvantages for both companies. The major concerns include tax considerations, liabilities, and the ease of completing the transaction. There are three basic transaction structures for US acquisitions: asset purchase transactions, stock purchase transactions, and merger transactions. Two important documents are used to delineate the M&A deal structuring process. They are the Term Sheet[1] and Letter of Intent (LOI).[2]

9.2 Asset Purchase Transaction

Where a business is acquired by way of an asset purchase transaction, the buyer (or a wholly owned subsidiary of the buyer) takes title to or ownership of specified assets of the target company and may agree to assume specified liabilities, but does not acquire ownership of the target corporation. An asset transaction allows the buyer to select the assets it desires to acquire and the liabilities it desires to assume. Put another way, all liabilities other than specified liabilities can be left behind with the target company. That said, depending on the circumstances, there could

F. Lessambo, *U.S. Mergers and Acquisitions*,
https://doi.org/10.1007/978-3-030-85735-6_9

be a risk that certain liabilities remained attached directly to certain assets purchased, and the buyer be responsible after sale.

9.2.1 *Advantages*

- The buyer can decide which assets to buy from the seller and which not to. The assets purchased are at the buyer's discretion and what buyer and seller agree upon. Most often, all of the assets are acquired and the selling company is left with the consideration, usually cash, and any remaining liabilities. The seller then either changes the name of the company and uses that entity for another purpose or liquidates the entity.
- In general, the buyer favors an asset purchase as it mitigates the possibility prior, and perhaps unknown, liabilities from the selling company will be their responsibility. In particular cases, the avoidance of liabilities is not clear-cut. For example, in certain jurisdictions, certain liabilities, e.g., environmental issues may penetrate any structure of an M&A transaction.
- The selling company continues as a corporate entity after the sale, containing the remaining unsold assets and liabilities.

9.2.2 *Disadvantages*

- The buyer may not be able to acquire non-transferable assets, e.g., goodwill.
- An asset acquisition may lead to high-impact tax costs for both the seller and the buyer. Double taxation occurs because the target company recognizes gain on the sale of assets and its stockholders recognize gain on liquidating dividends when the target company distributes net proceeds from the asset acquisition to them.
- Key contracts may not be assignable to the buyer in an asset purchase. An asset acquisition involving the purchase of a significant number of contracts can require the parties to obtain the written consent of numerous contract counterparties due to anti-assignment clauses.
- It may also take more time to close the deal, compared to other deal structures.

9.3 Stock Purchase Transaction

In a stock purchase transaction, the buyer simply purchases the stock of the selling company directly from shareholders in exchange for cash, the acquiring company's stock, other consideration, or a combination of the three. A stock acquisition is generally a simpler deal structure than an asset acquisition or a merger. Because the target company remains a going concern, there is no need to transfer assets or assign liabilities to the buyer. That is, the corporate status of the target company remains unchanged except that the buyer now owns the stock. In this case, the acquirer acquires all of the assets and all of the liabilities of the target company, unless agreed otherwise by the buyer and seller. In addition, in some cases, if the seller has valuable tax attributes, e.g., tax loss carry-forwards, the purchaser may be able to utilize them. Likewise, in a stock purchase transaction, the buyer becomes the owner of the stock of the target company, thereby indirectly acquiring all of the assets and liabilities of the target company. A stock transaction is feasible where there are a limited number of stockholders of the target company and all stockholders desire to sell to the buyer on the same terms and conditions.

9.3.1 Advantages of a Stock Purchase Acquisition

- An asset transaction generally will permit the acquisition premium to be allocated either to existing identifiable assets or to a new "goodwill" intangible and depreciated or amortized over time to offset taxable income.
- From the perspective of the target company's stockholders, a stock acquisition is generally more tax efficient than an asset acquisition because any gain results in a single level of tax at the stockholder level.
- Closing a stock purchase deal is less time-consuming since negotiations are less complicated.
- It may be less expensive.

9.3.2 Disadvantages of a Stock Purchase Acquisition

- Legal or financial liabilities may accompany a stock purchase acquisition.

- An asset acquisition normally is viewed as less desirable from the perspective of the target because it usually entails two layers of tax: one at the level of the target-seller and another at the shareholder level when the corporation distributes the proceeds.
- Uncooperative minority shareholders may also be a problem.
- From the buyer's perspective, a stock acquisition may not be as tax efficient as an asset acquisition because the buyer does not get a "stepped-up" basis in the target company's assets that can be used for higher depreciation and amortization deductions.

9.4 Merger Transaction

In a merger, two companies combine into one legal entity, with the surviving entity succeeding to all of the assets and liabilities of both entities. Every state has statutory and case law that governs the merger process and the laws of each state of incorporation of each entity participating in the merger require careful consideration. In general, these statutes require the parties to make detailed filings with the applicable states to consummate the merger. There are two basic merger structures: (i) the direct merger structure and (ii) the indirect merger structure. A direct merger occurs either when the target company and the buyer merge directly with the buyer surviving the merger (forward merger) or the target company surviving the merger (reverse merger). An indirect merger occurs when the target company merges with a subsidiary of the buyer with either the buyer's subsidiary surviving the merger (forward triangular merger) or the target company surviving the merger (reverse triangular merger). An indirect merger allows the buyer to keep the assets and liabilities of the target company separate from the buyer in a subsidiary, whereas in a direct merger, the assets and liabilities of the target company and the buyer are combined.

9.4.1 Direct Statutory Merger

In a Forward Merger structuring (a.k.a statutory merger), the target merges directly into the purchaser corporation. Thereafter, the target disappears while the purchaser survives. A direct statutory merger is a common merger in which the acquiring company acquires all of the target company's assets and liabilities. The target company then operates under the surviving company's name and is considered liquidated. All shareholders of the target company are compensated either for their shares or for hold shares in the surviving company.

- Forward Triangular Merger

In a forward triangular merger, also known as an indirect merger, the target company merges into a subsidiary of the acquiring company. This M&A deal structure normally takes place when the merger combines both cash and stock. Because the target company is merging into a subsidiary, rather than directly into the acquiring company, the acquiring company is protected from the target's liabilities.

With regard to shareholders, the acquisition subsidiary compensates the target's shareholders with stock, but up to 50% of their compensation can be in the form of cash and other non-stock options.

- Reverse Triangular Merger

The common reverse triangular merger, like a forward triangular merger, also shelters the acquiring company from the target's liabilities, because it is not a direct merger. However, the acquisition subsidiary in this case is not the surviving company. Instead, it purchases the target company and merges into the target company as a wholly owned subsidiary of the acquiring company. The buyer's stock or cash is issued to the target company's shareholders. It is because the surviving target company is preserved, so it keeps its business contracts and does not have to transfer its assets to the acquiring company, which may not be possible otherwise with anti-assignment clauses. This allows the acquiring company to have access and control of the target's business contracts, preserving the target's business continuity.

9.4.2 Indirect Statutory Merger

In an indirect statutory merger, a subsidiary of the purchasing company completes the acquisition on behalf of its parent company. The subsidiary company acquires all the assets and liabilities of the target company. The acquired company then becomes a fully owned subsidiary of the purchasing entity. After the acquisition, the target company is liquidated, and the buyer becomes the sole shareholder of the combined entity.

Notes

1. See: Chapter 2: Legal Documents.
2. Idem.

CHAPTER 10

Subsidiary Merger

10.1 General

The short-form merger statute, as enacted in 1937, authorized a parent corporation to merge with its wholly owned subsidiary by filing and recording a certificate evidencing the parent's ownership and its merger resolution. In 1957, the statute was expanded to include parent/subsidiary mergers where the parent company owns at least 90% of the stock of the subsidiary. The 1957 amendment also made it possible, for the first time and only in a short-form merger, to pay the minority cash for their shares, thereby eliminating their ownership interest in the company. In its current form, which has not changed significantly since 1957, 8 *Delaware.Corporate Law,* § 253 provides in relevant part:

(a) In any case in which at least 90% of the outstanding shares of each class of the stock of a corporation... is owned by another corporation..., the corporation having such stock ownership may ... merge the other corporation ... into itself... by executing, acknowledging and filing, in accordance with § 103 of this title, a certificate of such ownership and merger setting forth a copy of the resolution of its board of directors to so merge and the date of the adoption; provided, however, that in case the parent corporation shall not own all the outstanding stock of ... the subsidiary corporation[],... the resolution ... shall state the terms and conditions of the merger, including the securities, cash, property or rights

F. Lessambo, *U.S. Mergers and Acquisitions,*
https://doi.org/10.1007/978-3-030-85735-6_10

to be issued, paid delivered or granted by the surviving corporation upon surrender of each share of the subsidiary corporation....

* * *

(d) In the event that all of the stock of a subsidiary Delaware corporation... is not owned by the parent corporation immediately prior to the merger, the stockholders of the subsidiary Delaware corporation party to the merger shall have appraisal rights as set forth in Section 262 of this Title.

The 90% threshold is the relevant percentage for most states with the exception of a few states such as Alabama, Florida, and Montana in which these states have an 80% threshold.

10.2 Board Approval

In a short-form merger, there is no agreement of merger negotiated by two companies; there is only a unilateral act—a decision by the parent company that its 90% owned subsidiary shall no longer exist as a separate entity. The minority stockholders receive no advance notice of the merger; their directors do not consider or approve it; and there is no vote. Those who object are given the right to obtain fair value for their shares through appraisal. Once the board of directors approves the short-form merger, it creates a plan with a detailed definition of how the merger will proceed. That is, the contemplated effects of the merger to the company. Next, the plan is distributed to the shareholders to allow them to determine whether they want to proceed with the transaction. Once the majority of shareholders approve of the short-form merger, the legal proceedings begin.

10.3 Standard of Review

The parent corporation does not have to establish entire fairness, and absent fraud or illegality, the only recourse for a minority stockholder who is dissatisfied with the merger consideration is appraisal.

10.3.1 Duty of Full Disclosure

Although fiduciaries are not required to establish entire fairness in a short-form merger, the duty of full disclosure remains. Specifically, the company must notify the minority of the availability of appraisal rights and include a correct copy of the appraisal statute. Additionally, disclosure of the "information material to the decision of whether or not to seek appraisal is required." However, the parent need not provide all the information necessary for the stockholder to reach an independent determination of fair value. Information is material if there is "a substantial likelihood that the undisclosed information would significantly alter the total mix of information already provided." Omitted facts are not material simply because they might be helpful. A disclosure violation results in an irreparable injury, which may be remedied through quasi-appraisal. DCL Section 253 required that the notice includes a copy of the appraisal statute, and Delaware case law required that the acquisition transaction discloses in the notice of merger all information material to stockholders deciding whether or not to seek appraisal.

- In Berger v. Pubco Corp,[1] the Court of Chancery determined that the controlling stockholder had breached his disclosure duty in connection with a short-form merger by (i) sending the minority stockholders an outdated copy of the appraisal statute and (ii) failing to disclose all material facts relevant to the decision to accept the merger consideration or seek appraisal. The majority's disclosure had been sketchy in offering minority shareholders $20 for shares that had been trading in the market in the $12–$16 range.

The Chancery Court had ruled that there must be a quasi-appraisal action available for the minority after sufficient disclosure.

Delaware Supreme Court reversed the Delaware Court of Chancery's form of "quasi-appraisal" remedy and instructed the Court of Chancery to enter a quasi-appraisal remedy that includes all minority stockholders (except those that opt out) and to not require any minority stockholders to escrow a portion of their previously received merger consideration.

The Delaware Supreme Court held that

a "quasi-appraisal" remedy is an appropriate remedy in a short-form merger where greater than 90 percent stockholders breached its duty of disclose material information to the minority stockholders.

- In Re United Capital Corp.[2]

Plaintiff identifies numerous omitted facts he deems material. Specifically, he points to the exclusion of (1) the information used by the Special Committee to set the $32 per share merger price, (2) Petrocelli's rationale for his original offer, (3) specific financial information, including projections, (4) the extent to which cash and cash equivalents were working capital, (5) potential conflicts of two of the three purportedly independent members of the Special Committee, and (6) the identities of certain directors and a director's spouse who jointly owned an $8 million note with the Company.

10.4 Shareholders' Remedy: Quasi-Appraisal

In Rudd v. Brown, et al.,[3] the Delaware Court of Chancery dismissed Mr. Rudd's claim that the board members and the chief financial officer of Outerwall, Inc. disloyally pursued and disclosed a two-step merger, finding that Rudd failed to show that the defendants were conflicted, despite the potential that the director defendants would lose their seats in connection with a threatened proxy contest. Mr. Rudd claimed that directors failed to take reasonable efforts to maximize the value of the Company for the benefit of Outerwall's public stockholders, instead accepting grossly inadequate consideration. In addition, he also claimed that the directors failed to disclose material information concerning the acquisition, thus rendering the Company's stockholders unable to make an informed decision whether to tender their shares and whether to seek appraisal. Further, Rudd challenged the Company's disclosures on the ground that they contained material misrepresentations or omissions concerning Outerwall's financial projections.

In re United Capital Corp., Stockholders Litigation,[4] C.A. No. 11619-VCMR (Del. Ch. Jan. 4, 2017), the Delaware Court of Chancery dismissed a suit brought by plaintiff minority stockholders that sought a quasi-appraisal to remedy alleged breaches of the duty of disclosure in connection with the acquisition of United Capital Corp. via short-form merger. The Court concluded that Plaintiff had not adequately alleged that any omitted information was material to the decision to seek appraisal and that the duty of disclosure was not violated. The Court found that United Capital has provided much more financial information, including current, historical, and forward-looking information. The current and historical information includes, among other things, (1) audited, consolidated financial statements for the years 2013 and 2014, (2) unaudited, consolidated financial statements for six-month period ending in June 2015, (3) management's detailed analysis of the financials for the year 2014 and the six-month period ending in June 2015, and (4) the prices of recent buybacks of shares. More, the Court found that Plaintiff failed to explain why any additional information would alter the "total mix" of information available; instead, suggesting such information is helpful in performing an independent valuation of United Capital.

10.5 Defense Against Monetary Damages

- In actions for monetary damages against the directors of Delaware corporations with a Section 102(b)(7) charter provision, a shareholder's complaint must allege well-pled facts that, if true, implicate breaches of loyalty or good faith. That is, a plaintiff seeking only monetary damages must plead non-exculpated claims against a director who is protected by an exculpatory charter provision to survive a motion to dismiss, regardless of the underlying standard of review for the board's conduct—be it *Revlon*, *Unocal*, the entire fairness standard, or the business judgment rule.

10.6 The Directors' Exculpatory Defense

Delaware courts have consistently held that the adoption of a charter provision, in accordance with Section 102(b)(7), bars the recovery of monetary damages from directors for a successful shareholder claim that is based exclusively upon establishing a violation of the duty of care. Under Revlon scrutiny, an exculpatory charter provision shields defendant directors from monetary liability where the underlying claims for a breach of fiduciary duties in conducting the sale are based only on duty of care violations. Thus, plaintiffs challenging a transaction under Revlon and seeking monetary damages, like Rudd here, must plead facts sufficient to state a non-exculpated fiduciary duty claim.

One way to state a non-exculpated claim against a director protected by a 102(b)(7) provision is to plead facts for each director "supporting a rational inference that the director harbored self-interest adverse to the stockholder's interest, acted to advance the self-interest of an interested party from whom they could not be presumed to act independently, or acted in bad faith. The same standard governs disclosure claims. When asserting a disclosure claim for damages against directors post-close, a plaintiff must allege facts making it reasonably conceivable that there has been a non-exculpated breach of fiduciary duty by the board in failing to make a material disclosure. Likewise, when an exculpation provision under 8Del. C. § 102(b)(7) shields a board from duty-of-care claims, this means a plaintiff must demonstrate that a majority of the board was not disinterested or independent, or that the board was otherwise disloyal because it failed to act in good faith, unfailing to make the material disclosure."

10.7 Types of Subsidiary Merger

The following are the two main types of subsidiary mergers:

10.7.1 Forward Triangular Merger

A forward triangular merger is an indirect merger where a subsidiary of the purchasing company completes the acquisition on behalf of its parent company. The subsidiary company acquires all the assets and liabilities of the target company. The acquired company then becomes a fully owned subsidiary of the purchasing entity. After the acquisition, the target company is liquidated, and the buyer becomes the sole shareholder of the combined entity. One of the reasons why buyers prefer a forward triangular merger is that it gives them more flexibility in terms of purchasing the target company. Buyers can use a combination of both cash and stock. Half of the consideration used to pay the target company's shareholders must be at least 50% stock of the acquirer. If the consideration for the transaction were 100% cash, it would make the transaction taxable.

On the downside, forward triangular mergers are less preferred than reverse triangular mergers due to issues regarding access to the target company's licenses and authorizations. The properties will need to be reassessed, and some third parties may withhold consent to the acquirer gaining use of the target company's contracts, licenses, and authorizations. The acquiring entity may incur additional costs in order to be granted consent to the rights of the licenses and assignment of contracts.

10.7.2 Reverse Triangular Merger

In a Reverse Triangular Merger, a buyer acquires a target company by forming a subsidiary to merge with and into a target company. The target company assumes all of the merger subsidiary's assets, rights, and liabilities by operation of law, and the merger subsidiary ceases to exist as a separate entity while the target company survives the merger and becomes a subsidiary of the buyer. A reverse triangular merger retains the selling entity and liquidates the shell company created for executing the acquisition. The acquired entity continues its regular operations as a subsidiary of the buyer, and the acquiring entity will not need to sign new contracts, licenses, and authorizations. A reverse triangular merger can be structured tax-free if the acquiring entity uses its stock to acquire 80% of the target company's stock. That is, cash and other non-stock consideration must not exceed 20% of the total consideration paid if the buyer wants to enjoy a tax-free acquisition transaction.

10.8 Shareholders' Appraisal Right

The ability of stockholders to seek and recover statutory appraisal of the value of their shares when dissenting from the consideration offered in a merger transaction has been restrained by recent amendments to the Delaware General Corporation Law (DGCL) and several Delaware court decisions. Appraisal is available in a merger or consolidation governed by Section 262 only for the stock of a "constituent corporation." Where a merger subsidiary merely functions as an intermediary entity, solely formed to facilitate the merger, its "constituent corporation" status is not imputed to its parent corporation. Section 262 (b)(i) of the DGCL provides that no appraisal rights shall be available for any shares of stock of the constituent corporation surviving a merger if the merger did not require for its approval the vote of the stockholders of the surviving corporation.

- *Meso Scale Diagnostics, LLC v. Roche Diagnostics GmbH*[5]

- In 2007, Roche Diagnostics GmbH ("Roche") as a means for Roche to acquire BioVeris's intellectual property rights acquired BioVeris Corp. ("BioVeris"). Under the terms of these intellectual property rights, the consent of Meso Scale was required to assign such rights "by operation of law or otherwise."
- The transaction was structured as a reverse triangular merger with Roche forming an acquisition subsidiary to merge with and into BioVeris, as the surviving corporation.
- In 2010, Meso Scale filed a complaint with the Court alleging, among other things, that Roche's 2007 acquisition of BioVeris, without the consent of Meso Scale, resulted in a breach of BioVeris's intellectual property rights because the acquisition constituted an assignment of BioVeris's intellectual property rights by operation of law.
- In its recent decision granting summary judgment in favor of Roche, the Court did not find Meso Scale's arguments to be persuasive nor Meso Scale's interpretation of the anti-assignment provision to be reasonable. The Court relied on an examination of the parties' intent while drafting the anti-assignment provision at issue, and how statutory, juridical, and practical precedent may have informed them.
- The Court started its analysis by stating that, as a matter of principle, mergers do not result in an assignment by operation of law of assets that began as property of the surviving entity and continued to be such after the merger.
- The Court was not persuaded by Meso Scale's claim that Roche's acquisition was essentially nothing more than an assignment of BioVeris's intellectual property rights to Roche.
- The Court noted that Meso Scale's claim ignores Delaware's long-standing doctrine of independent legal significance, which applies in situations where deals were structured to avoid consent rights. That doctrine holds that the "mere fact that the result of actions taken under one section may be the same as the result of action taken under another section does not require that the legality of the result must be tested by the requirements of the second section."
- Meso Scale cited an unpublished 1991 decision of the United States District Court for the Northern District of California in *SQL Solutions, Inc. v. Oracle Corp.* that did conclude that a reverse triangular merger resulted in an assignment by operation of law. The *SQL Solutions* court further stated, more generally, that "an assignment or

transfer of rights does occur through a change in the legal form of ownership of a business."
- The Court brushed up that argument and held that "both stock acquisitions and reverse triangular mergers involve changes in legal ownership, and the law should reflect parallel results."

- *City of North Miami Beach General Employees' Retirement Plan v. Dr. Pepper Snapple Group, Inc.*[6]

City of North Miami Beach General Employees' Retirement Plan v. Dr Pepper Snapple Group, Inc., No. 0227, decided 6/1/18. The Delaware Chancery Court held that the stockholders of the parent corporation of a subsidiary involved in a merger were not entitled to appraisal rights under Sect. 262 of the General Corporation Law because the parent was not a constituent to the merger and the stockholders were not relinquishing their stock.

Legal Insights

I. Glassman v. Unocal Expl. Corp.—777 A.2d 242 (Del. 2001):

In a short-form merger conducted pursuant to Del. Code Ann. tit. 8, § 253, the parent corporation did not have to establish entire fairness, and, absent fraud or illegality, appraisal was the only recourse for minority stockholders who were dissatisfied with the merger consideration. The determination of fair value must be based on all relevant factors, including damages and elements of future value, where appropriate.

Facts:

- Unocal Corporation was an earth resources company primarily engaged in the exploration for and production of crude oil and natural gas.
- At the time of the merger, Unocal owned approximately 96% of the stock of Unocal Exploration Corporation ("UXC"), an oil and gas company operating in and around the Gulf of Mexico.
- In December 1991, the boards of Unocal and UXC appointed Special Committees to consider a possible merger.
- On February 24, 1992, Unocal and UXC announced the merger, and it was effected, pursuant to 8 *Delaware Corporation Law.* § 253, on May 2, 1992.

- The Notice of Merger and Prospectus stated the terms of the merger and advised the former UXC stockholders of their appraisal rights.
- Glassman, a subsidiary corporation's minority shareholders, filed a class action against Unocal Expl. Corp., the parent corporation and its directors, alleging that the directors breached their fiduciary duties of entire fairness and full disclosure.
- The Court of Chancery held that the minority shareholders' exclusive remedy was appraisal.
- The shareholders appealed, and the Supreme Court confirmed the Chancery Court holding.

I .*Berger v. Pubco Corp.*, No. 509, 2008 (Del. July 9, 2009):

The Court held that the proper remedy for disclosure violations in a short-form merger is a quasi-appraisal action on behalf of an automatic class of all minority stockholders with no escrow requirement. Moreover, although fiduciaries are not required to establish entire fairness in a short-form merger, the duty of full disclosure remains. Where the only choice for the minority stockholders is whether to accept the merger consideration or seek appraisal, they must be given all the factual information that is material to that decision.

Facts:

- Sometime before October 12, 2007, Kanner decided that Pubco should "go private."
- To proceed, as the owner of over 90% of Pubco's outstanding shares, Kanner formed a wholly owned shell subsidiary, Pubco Acquisition, Inc., and transferred his Pubco shares to that entity to effect the merger.
- In that merger, which took place on October 12, 2007, Pubco's minority stockholders received $20 cash per share.
- In November 2007, Barbara Berger, a Pubco minority shareholder, received a written notice from Pubco, advising that Pubco's controlling shareholder had effected a short-form merger, and that Barbara Berger and the other minority stockholders were being cashed out for $ 20 per share
- The Notice explained that shareholder approval was not required for the merger to become effective, and that the minority stockholders

had the right to seek an appraisal. Pubco further attached to the Notice a copy of the appraisal statute.

- On December 14, 2007, Barbara Berger initiated the present lawsuit as a class action on behalf of all Pubco minority stockholders, claiming that the class was entitled to receive the difference between the $ 20 per share paid to each class member and the fair value of his or her shares, irrespective whether any class member demanded appraisal.
- In its Opinion, the Court of Chancery addressed two issues: (1) Whether the Notice contained material misstatements or omissions that constituted disclosure violations, and (2) if so, what was the appropriate remedy.
- The Court of Chancery held that because the notice of merger did not disclose material facts, the minority shareholders electing an appraisal of their shares were entitled to opt in to the proceeding, and escrow part of the consideration received for their shares.
- The Supreme Court held the remedy ordered was not appropriate: (i) The shareholders should not have been ordered to opt in because this imposed a burden on them, while it did not burden the corporation to automatically include them in the class, with an option to opt out, which was the remedy that should have been ordered and (ii) they should not have been required to put part of the consideration they received for their shares in escrow because the quasi-appraisal remedy that operated in the fairest and most balanced way and that best effectuated the legislative intent underlying Del. Code Ann. tit. 8, § 253 was the one that did not require this, and it was not inequitable in long-form mergers.
- The Court held that in cases where the corporation does not comply with the disclosure requirement mandated by *Glassman*, the quasi-appraisal remedy that operates in the fairest and most balanced way and that best effectuates the legislative intent underlying Section 253 is the one that does not require the minority shareholders seeking a recovery of fair value to escrow a portion of the merger proceeds they received. We hold, for these reasons, that the quasi-appraisal remedy ordered by the Court of Chancery was legally erroneous in the circumstances presented here.

Notes

1. In Berger v. Pubco Corp., No. 509, 208 (Del., July 9, 2009).
2. In Re United Capital Corp., (Consolidated Stockholders Litigation) C.A. No. 11619-VCMR.
3. In Rudd v. Brown, et al., C.A. No. 2019–0775 MTZ (Del. Ch. Sept. 11, 2020),
4. In re United Capital Corp., Stockholders Litigation, C.A. No. 11619-VCMR (Del. Ch. Jan. 4, 2017).
5. *Meso Scale Diagnostics, LLC v. Roche Diagnostics GmbH, C.A.* No. 5589-VCP (Del. Ch. 2011).
6. *City of North Miami Beach General Employees' Retirement Plan v. Dr Pepper Snapple Group, Inc.*, No. 0227, decided 6/1/18.

CHAPTER 11

The Impact of U.S. Tax Code on Mergers and Acquisitions

11.1 General

We are witnessing a huge upswing in cross-border mergers and acquisitions activity—$1.3 trillion in deals in 2014 alone, with foreign takeovers of U.S. companies accounting for $275 billion of that total. This is double the value of takeovers in 2013, and every expectation is that the boom will continue throughout 2015. This increasing trend merits an examination about the causes of this merger impact, and the larger impact on jobs, tax revenue, and innovation.

A recent analysis by Ernst & Young found that, from 2004 to 2013, foreign buyers acquired $179 billion more of U.S. companies than we acquired of theirs. Additionally, data provider Dealogic reports that the gross value of foreign takeovers of U.S. companies doubled last year to $275 billion and, at the current rate, will surpass $400 billion this year. These takeovers reflect thousands of U.S. companies leaving American shores.

11.2 M&A Motivations

Businesses buy and merge with other businesses primarily because of "ownership advantages"—the means by which an acquirer expects to create new value. Those advantages may take a number of forms. An acquirer might believe it can boost a target company's profits through

F. Lessambo, *U.S. Mergers and Acquisitions*,
https://doi.org/10.1007/978-3-030-85735-6_11

cost-cutting, improve sales through better marketing, or enhance productivity by integrating complementary technologies. An acquirer expects that its ownership advantages will increase the target firm's future cash flow, thus "enabling the acquirer to outbid the reservation price of the initial owner[s] and increase the likelihood that the deal takes place." In other words, ownership advantages allow the acquirer to pay a premium—more than the target firm is valued by the market as a whole.[1]

11.3 Tax Synergies

There are tax synergies to be realized through the integration of newly acquired businesses into a preexisting structure. Those benefits generally derive from two sources: (i) the use of debt to finance the acquisitions; and (ii) the integration of the intellectual property of the acquired companies into the preexisting corporate structure.[2]

- Debt financing

Using a third party borrowing to finance the acquisitions provides a tax benefit in the form of deductible interest expense paid by U.S. entities within the acquirer corporate group. The bias that the U.S. tax code—like many tax codes—provides in favor of debt financing (as compared to equity financing) is well known and is certainly not unique to non-U.S. parented companies. However, it is a feature of the tax system that we benefit from—and that provides us with tax synergies in the context of acquisitions given our preference for financing those acquisitions with debt.[3]

- Intangible property planning

As the IP has become the most important asset in many companies, careful holding of IP in terms of where to fund the ongoing development of that intellectual property, and where to locate the attendant functions related to the commercialization of our products that embody that intellectual property is of great consideration along the M&A process. The applicable tax rates in various jurisdictions are of course a key consideration in the decisions we make regarding where to hold our intellectual property portfolio. To the extent that the ownership and ongoing development of intellectual property are moved outside of the U.S., the costs associated with that development are not borne in the U.S. and thus are not tax deductible.

11.4 Case Studies

Valeant has been able to acquire successively (i) Medicis Pharmaceutical Corporation (2012); (ii) Bausch & Lomb Holding Incorporation (2013); and (iii) Salix Pharmaceuticals, Ltd. (2015).

Valeant Pharmaceuticals International, Inc., is a Canadian-based multinational specialty pharmaceutical company. The company has operations across six continents, with activity in both developed and emerging markets. Its products include over both-the-counter and prescription drugs, with a focus in dermatology, eye health, neurology, gastrointestinal medicine, and consumer health care. Originally, a U.S. corporation based in California, Valeant merged with Canada's largest publicly traded drugmaker, Biovail Corporation, in 2010, with Biovail surviving as the parent. The combined company moved its global headquarters to Ontario, Canada before relocating to Quebec in 2012. After the acquisition, former Biovail shareholders owned 50.5% of the new firm, while former Valeant shareholders received 49.5%, along with an additional cash dividend.

11.4.1 The Acquisition of Medicis Pharmaceutical Corporation (2012)

In December 2012, Valeant acquired Medicis, a U.S. pharmaceutical company headquartered in Scottsdale, Arizona, for U.S. $2.6 billion (or $44 per share) in an all-cash deal. The $44 price per share paid by Valeant represented a 39% premium on Medicis's closing share price before the acquisition was announced. Valeant explained the acquisition primarily as a means of expanding its reach and offerings in dermatology. Valeant and its target had dramatically different tax profiles. Before the acquisition, Medicis had a U.S. cash effective tax rate of 30.3% in 2010 and 25% in 2011. Medicis had no significant non-U.S. income. By contrast, Valeant had a U.S. cash effective tax rate of 0% and 0.6% in 2010 and 2011, respectively, and a worldwide cash effective tax rate of 5.9% and 4.5% in 2010 and 2011, respectively.[4]

In an August 2013 presentation to the Valeant board, Valeant executives forecasted that it would be possible to achieve a "20% effective tax rate post acquisition" on legacy Medicis profits. Valeant projected that it could significantly enhance its return on the Medicis acquisition by integrating it into a corporate group based in Canada. When evaluated at a tax rate close to the U.S. statutory rate, the net present value of the Medicis deal gains (at the ultimate acquisition price of $44/share) was $981 million. That value increased by 75% (or $740 million) to $1.72 billion when viewed through the lens of a foreign acquirer capable of reducing the target company's cash effective tax rate to 20%. Similarly, the internal rate of return on the Medicis acquisition rose from 14 to 17% when Valeant's tax-planning advantages were accounted for. And Valeant determined that its investment in Medicis would pay for itself faster—within 7.2 years rather than 9.1 years—at a 20% tax rate.[5]

Valeant "anticipated that its effort to integrate [Medicis into Valeant] would yield significant savings," but it did not specifically quantify the savings. Post-acquisition tax savings, however, can be approximated based on Valeant's projection of the achievable effective tax rate for Medicis done as part of the deal analysis. Assuming a cash effective tax rate of 20% post-acquisition compared to a 36% rate, the acquisition by Valeant could yield approximately $680 million in tax savings over 10 years.[6]

A. The IP transfers

Before the acquisition, all of Medicis's intellectual property was held in the U.S., and all royalties were earned in the U.S. Within four months of the acquisition, Valeant transferred Medicis's intellectual property portfolio to low-tax foreign jurisdictions, with the exception of products that Valeant had sold or discontinued. It achieved this through a multi-step process. To simplify, the newly acquired Medicis granted Valeant-Canada a license to all its intellectual property. Valeant-Canada sub-licensed that newly transferred Medicis intellectual property to other entities, ultimately consolidating the rights to Medicis's patents in Valeant's Irish subsidiary (Valeant Holdings Ireland or VHI) and (for a short time) Valeant's U.S. group.[7]

The object of these intellectual property transfers was to shift abroad the upside of any future appreciation in the value of Medicis's property. To understand why, it is important to note that transferring intellectual property outside the country does have a cost. Under section 482 of the tax code, Valeant's foreign affiliates were required to compensate Valeant's U.S. group for the intellectual property transfer at an arms-length rate—which results in taxable income in the U.S. To simplify, that transaction must be priced to reflect the value of the intellectual property at the time of the transfer. Consequently, if the transferred intellectual property later appreciates, the accretion will be taxed at the lower foreign rate. If the intellectual property unexpectedly depreciates, the guarantee royalty payment mandated by section 482 will cause a loss.[8]

Valeant essentially placed a bet that transferring Medicis's intellectual property overseas would be worth the upfront tax cost. To comply with section 482, when Valeant transferred Medicis's intellectual property abroad, it set up tiered royalties payments (at rates between 20 and 35% depending on the level of net sales for each product) that Valeant's non-U.S. affiliates must pay to Valeant's U.S. group in exchange for the transfer; those payments are taxable in the U.S. Since 2013, Valeant's non-U.S. affiliates have paid $156 million in U.S.-taxable Medicis royalties to the U.S. group.

Through the intellectual property transfers, Valeant ensured that (except for the tiered royalties described above) future income derived from Medicis's intellectual property would be earned by entities outside the U.S. In the first full year following the acquisition, while it received the inbound royalty payments described above, Valeant's U.S. group also paid significant royalties to Valeant Pharmaceuticals Luxembourg (VPL) and Valeant-Canada for use of transferred Medicis intellectual property. Those outbound royalty payments are then taxed at the lower Canadian or Luxembourg rates.[9]

Valeant consolidated much of its worldwide intellectual property in a single principal company—Valeant Holdings Ireland—and converted its U.S. entities into essentially limited-risk distributors and contract manufacturers. Under that arrangement, VHI contracts with Valeant affiliates (including some U.S. entities) to manufacture Medicis products. A member of Valeant's U.S. group, VPNA, then buys the finished product from VHI and handles product sales, marketing, and distribution in the U.S.82 As a result, apart from the return on those services and the tiered royalties required under section 482, Valeant's Irish subsidiary now earns substantially all the income on worldwide sales of Medicis products; Valeant's U.S. group shares in part of those profits through its equity interest in VHI.

B. The intercompany debt

The Valeant-Canada parent did not issue the Medicis acquisition debt, and consequently it has not resulted in significant outbound interest payments to low-tax jurisdictions. Valeant's non-U.S. affiliates did, however, guarantee the Medicis acquisition debt. As a result, Valeant's U.S. group makes significant outbound guarantee fee payments. In 2013 and 2014, Valeant's U.S. group made $19.5 million in guarantee fee payments to non-U.S. related parties in connection with the Medicis acquisition debt, and those payments will continue for the life of the corresponding loans. The outbound guarantee fees are deductible for U.S. federal tax purposes.[10]

11.4.2 The Acquisition of Bausch & Lomb Holding Incorporation (2013)

On August 5, 2013, Valeant acquired Bausch & Lomb, one of the world's largest producers of eye health products. The acquisition was completed for $8.7 billion in cash, with $4.5 billion paid to the target's owner, the private equity firm Warburg Pincus, and the remaining $4.2 billion used to pay down the target's outstanding debt. Headquartered in Rochester, New York, Bausch & Lomb initially filed to go public before Valeant acquired it, reporting $3.03 billion in annual sales in 2012.88 by further expanding Valeant's ophthalmology offerings and facilitating an expansion into China, Valeant anticipated the acquisition would create a "global eye health platform with estimated pro forma 2013 net revenue of more than $3.5 billion."

Prior to the acquisition, Bausch & Lomb boasted a significant international presence; the company had manufacturing in nine countries and sales in more than 100. In 2012, more than 60% of its revenue was from outside the U.S., and the company's growth plans contemplated expansion in new markets, including Argentina, India, and Japan. At the time of the acquisition, Bausch & Lomb had $187 million in un-repatriated overseas earnings. With a projected 32% worldwide effective tax rate at the time of the acquisition, Bausch & Lomb's future tax burden stood in sharp contrast to Valeant's single-digit worldwide rate and ability to repatriate international earnings without additional taxes.[11]

In evaluating the acquisition, Valeant again analyzed the extent to which it could reduce rates on Bausch & Lomb's worldwide income by integrating the company into Valeant's Canada-based corporate group. In a May 2013 presentation to the company's Board, Valeant executives presented the results of that analysis. Valeant compared the economics of the Bausch & Lomb acquisition using two potential tax rates: 36% (close to Bausch & Lomb's projected steady-state rate) and 20% (the worldwide cash tax rate Valeant believed it could achieve post-acquisition). Again, the analysis showed that the tax advantages available to Valeant would make the Bausch & Lomb acquisition significantly more attractive along several key deal metrics.[12]

Valeant determined that its investment in Bausch & Lomb would pay for itself in a shorter time period—8 years rather than 9.7 years—at a 20% tax rate.[13]

In financial models prepared prior to the acquisition, Valeant analyzed available tax planning in greater detail. The company ran three alternative tax-planning scenarios through its proprietary model. The most tax-efficient scenario was labeled "Alt 6." The Alt 6 scenario contemplated a transfer of all intellectual property to Valeant Holdings Ireland through a guaranteed license, as well as a "push down" of $3.5 billion in debt to Valeant's U.S. group. Valeant projected that the Alt 6 strategy would reduce Bausch & Lomb's average cash effective tax rate to 17.1% through 2023 and achieve a cash effective tax rate of 9.9% for the combined entity. Valeant projected that the "status quo" for Bausch & Lomb would result in a 10-year tax bill of $5.13 billion, while integration into Valeant would reduce that tax bill to $2.99 billion—for a tax savings of $2.13 billion. Those projected tax savings rise to $3.6 billion when deductions attributable to Valeant's intercompany acquisition debt are accounted for.

Valeant's tax planning appears to have had a significant effect on Bausch & Lomb's tax profile. The target company was integrated into a corporate group with a U.S. cash effective tax rate of 0.8% and worldwide cash effective tax rate of 3.3% in the first year following the acquisition. Post-acquisition tax rates for Bausch & Lomb are not available because the target company was entirely integrated into Valeant rather than transformed into a subsidiary. The effect of Valeant's integration of Bausch & Lomb, however, is reflected to some extent by a comparison of Bausch & Lomb's projected non-GAAP tax rate of 32% (2013 and 2014) with Valeant's post-acquisition cash tax rates. Valeant's U.S. cash effective tax rate remained under 1% in the first full year following the acquisition, and its worldwide cash effective tax rate ticked up from 3.1 to 3.3%.[14]

A. IP transfers

Before the acquisition, approximately 75% of Bausch & Lomb's intellectual property was located in the U.S. Within five months of the acquisitions, Valeant moved Bausch & Lomb's entire intellectual property portfolio to Ireland. It achieved this through a multi-step process. First, Valeant transferred and consolidated its ownership interests in VPL, Bausch & Lomb S.a.r.l. (a Luxembourg subsidiary), and certain other non-U.S. entities into its Irish subsidiary VHI.

Second, Valeant's U.S. entities (including Bausch & Lomb U.S.) granted two U.S. Valeant holding companies a fully paid-up exclusive license to their entire intellectual property portfolio, in exchange for shares in the holding companies.

Third, the two Valeant U.S. holding companies, in turn, granted VHI a fully paid-up exclusive license to their intellectual property, in exchange for equity in VHI.

Because that equity in VHI served as compensation for the transfer of intellectual property to a related party, Valeant was required under section 482 of the tax code to ensure the interest corresponded to the arms-length value of the transferred intellectual property at the time of the sale. Going forward, Valeant's U.S. holding companies receive a share of worldwide income earned by VHI, and that income is taxable in the U.S. The practical result of these transfers is that all income on non-U.S. sales of Bausch & Lomb products is earned outside the U.S. tax "net," except for the U.S. share of VHI income. In addition, the income from U.S. sales of Bausch & Lomb products is now limited to the routine return on product sales, marketing, and distribution in the U.S. and manufacturing (to the extent it is performed in the U.S.), plus the U.S. share of VHI income. Bausch & Lomb's U.S. entities now function essentially as a "contract manufacturer, providing manufacturing services to other members of the Valeant group." VPNA (a U.S. Valeant subsidiary) serves as a limited-risk distributor, which purchases finished product from other members of the Valeant group for distribution in the U.S. Consequently, all income generated by Bausch & Lomb's intellectual property is sourced and taxed abroad, with the exception of the U.S. shares of VHI income described above and the fees for contract manufacturing and distribution functions.[15]

It is important to note that Valeant Holdings Ireland is now the company's principal "risk taker" with respect to intellectual property. VHI bears the risks and costs associated with the ongoing development and exploitation of the licensed Medicis and Bausch & Lomb intellectual property. But VHI also will earn the rewards. If Valeant is successful in its plans to enhance the profitability of Medicis and Bausch & Lomb's intellectual property, the lion's share of those increased or "synergized" profits will flow to VHI.

B. Inter-company debt

Valeant pushed down $2.4 billion of the acquisition debt from its foreign affiliates to a Delaware subsidiary (VPI-Delaware), thereby creating a stream of deductible interest payments that have significantly reduced Bausch & Lomb's U.S. tax base.

Specifically, Valeant-Canada issued an aggregate $7.3 billion in debt financing from third-party banks. Valeant-Canada then made an interest-free loan of $3.1 billion to a Luxembourg subsidiary, Biovail International S.a.r.l., which in turn made an interest-bearing loan (at 6%) of $2.4 billion to VPI-Delaware.

The result of this intercompany lending is evident in the rise in Valeant-U.S.'s tax-deductible, outbound related-party interest payments. In the two years preceding the Bausch & Lomb acquisition, Valeant's U.S. group made an average of $219,000 per quarter in related-party interest payments. In the first full year following the acquisition, those payments swelled to $59.9 million per quarter—a 273-fold increase. To date, Valeant's U.S. group has made $320.2 million in interest payments on the Bausch & Lomb acquisition debt to Biovail International S.a.r.l. and projects another $375 million in interest payments through the first quarter of 2017; those payments will continue through the life of the loan. The interest payments are fully deductible in the U.S. and subject to no U.S. federal withholding taxes. Only a portion of the interest income received by Valeant in Luxembourg is taxable—at single-digit tax rates.[16]

11.4.3 The Acquisition of Salix Pharmaceuticals, Ltd (2015)

Founded in 1989, Salix Pharmaceuticals was a North Carolina-based pharmaceutical company specializing in gastrointestinal health. In 2013, the company had $933.8 million in revenues108 and a market capitalization of more than $5.47 billion. With an effective tax rate hovering in the high 30s to low 40s, however, the company actively sought opportunities to relocate to a lower-tax jurisdiction.

On July 9, 2014, Salix announced that it had agreed to buy an Irish subsidiary of the Italian-based pharmaceutical firm Cosmo Pharmaceuticals SpA for $2.7 billion in stock. The planned deal was to be structured as an inversion, placing the combined company's headquarters in Ireland. If the transaction was approved, Salix shareholders would own slightly less than 80% of the new firm; that ownership percentage shielded the deal from one of the anti-inversion provisions contained in section 7874 of the tax code, which treats inverted corporations as domestic corporations when shareholders of the U.S. Company own 80% or more of the new entity. Salix Chief Executive Officer Carolyn Logan specifically noted that the deal would "greatly enhance" the company's ability to compete for new acquisitions.[17]

Valeant and other interested acquirers then stepped in. Within months, in February 2015, Valeant announced that it had agreed to acquire Salix for $158 per share. The companies later revised the terms to $173 per share, for a total enterprise value of approximately $15.8 billion. The acquisition price represented a greater than 40% premium over Salix's share price before the acquisition was announced.

Before the acquisition, Salix projected that its U.S. cash effective tax rate would level out at 38% in 2017 and beyond; market analysts similarly expected Salix's future effective tax rate to hover in the "mid/high 30% range." By contrast, Valeant had a U.S. cash effective tax rate of 0% and 0.8% in 2013 and 2014, respectively, and a worldwide cash effective tax rate of 3.1% and 3.3% in 2013 and 2014, respectively.[18]

Valeant again evaluated the deal in light of potential tax savings. It assumed the applicable 36% statutory rate applied to the Salix acquisition. Nevertheless, because Valeant was uncertain precisely what rate it could achieve post-acquisition, it evaluated the deal based on two possible achievable tax rates, 5 and 10%. Valeant projected that it could significantly enhance the economics of the Salix acquisition by drawing on its non-U.S. tax profile. Once again, Valeant projected that the only way to hit its goal of 20% internal rate of return was by reducing the target's tax rate through integrating it into a Canada-based corporate group. Assuming a share price of $160, Valeant projected that its internal rate of return would be 15.6% at a 36% tax rate, which would jump to a 22.4% return at a 5% tax rate.[19]

Valeant estimated that the "aggregate tax savings" from its post-acquisition tax planning "would be approximately $562 million over five years" in nominal dollars. The immediate tools for achieving those savings entailed the transfer of intellectual property outside the U.S. tax net and the use of intercompany lending.

A. IP transfers

Prior to the acquisition, all but an insignificant portion of Salix's intellectual property was held in the U.S. Valeant now plans to transfer most legacy Salix intellectual property to Ireland. Specifically, Salix will license certain intellectual property to VHI, which acts as a principal for the global Valeant group. As compensation for the transfer, VHI "will pay a running royalty to Salix calculated as a percentage of third-party net sales," and it will acquire an option to purchase that intellectual property outright from Salix in the future. The royalties paid under that license will be "determined on a product-by-product basis based on analysis of the current value and risk profile" of each product. Because Salix will become a member of Valeant's U.S. consolidated group, however, Salix's taxable income associated with the intellectual property transfer going forward "will be offset with interest expense and other tax attributes.[20]"

The practical result of this restructuring is that VHI will contract with related parties and third parties to manufacture Salix products and then sell those products as finished goods to a member of Valeant's U.S. group, VPNA. VPNA will earn a return only on its product distribution, sales, and marketing activities. As a result, Valeant will source all income from Salix products to Ireland, except for royalties that VHI pays to its U.S. group for use of Salix intellectual property based on the value at the time of transfer. As with Medicis's and Bausch & Lomb's intellectual property, if Valeant is successful in its plans to enhance the profitability of Salix intellectual property, the lion's share of those increased or "synergized" profits will flow to VHI and be taxed at the lower Irish rate.[21]

B. Intercompany debt

Valeant structured the Salix acquisition debt in a manner that will significantly reduce Valeant's U.S. tax base. Valeant-Canada raised $15.2 billion in debt financing from third parties to support the Salix acquisition.

Valeant then made an interest-free loan of $16.5 billion to VFL (Luxembourg). VFL, in turn, made six intercompany loans totaling $16.5 billion to VPI Delaware at an average interest rate of approximately 6.2%. Valeant projects that, from the first quarter of 2015 through the first quarter of 2017, it will make $1.67 billion in interest payments on the Salix debt to VFL; those payments are scheduled to continue until the maturity date of each loan (ranging from 2021 to 2025). To date, Valeant's interest payments on the Salix acquisition debt have been fully deductible in the U.S. and subject to no U.S. federal withholding taxes.127 Only a portion of the interest income received by Valeant in Luxembourg is taxable—at single-digit tax rates.

Notes

1. US Senate Investigations Committee (July 30, 2015): Impact of the U.S. Tax Code on the Market for Corporate Control and Jobs, Majority Staff report, p. 4.
2. Schiller Howard testimony before the US Senate Committee, p. 10.
3. Idem.
4. US Senate Investigations Committee (July 30, 2015): Impact of the U.S. Tax Code on the Market for Corporate Control and Jobs, Majority Staff report, p. 16.
5. US Senate Investigations Committee (July 30, 2015): Impact of the U.S. Tax Code on the Market for Corporate Control and Jobs, Majority Staff report, p. 17.
6. US Senate Investigations Committee (July 30, 2015): Impact of the U.S. Tax Code on the Market for Corporate Control and Jobs, Majority Staff report, p. 18.
7. US Senate Investigations Committee (July 30, 2015): Impact of the U.S. Tax Code on the Market for Corporate Control and Jobs, Majority Staff report, p. 19.
8. US Senate Investigations Committee (July 30, 2015): Impact of the U.S. Tax Code on the Market for Corporate Control and Jobs, Majority Staff report, p. 19.
9. US Senate Investigations Committee (July 30, 2015): Impact of the U.S. Tax Code on the Market for Corporate Control and Jobs, Majority Staff report, p. 20.

10. US Senate Investigations Committee (July 30, 2015): Impact of the U.S. Tax Code on the Market for Corporate Control and Jobs, Majority Staff report, p. 21.
11. US Senate Investigations Committee (July 30, 2015): Impact of the U.S. Tax Code on the Market for Corporate Control and Jobs, Majority Staff report, p. 22.
12. Idem.
13. US Senate Investigations Committee (July 30, 2015): Impact of the U.S. Tax Code on the Market for Corporate Control and Jobs, Majority Staff report, p. 23.
14. US Senate Investigations Committee (July 30, 2015): Impact of the U.S. Tax Code on the Market for Corporate Control and Jobs, Majority Staff report, p. 24.
15. US Senate Investigations Committee (July 30, 2015): Impact of the U.S. Tax Code on the Market for Corporate Control and Jobs, Majority Staff report, p. 25.
16. US Senate Investigations Committee (July 30, 2015): Impact of the U.S. Tax Code on the Market for Corporate Control and Jobs, Majority Staff report, p. 26.
17. US Senate Investigations Committee (July 30, 2015): Impact of the U.S. Tax Code on the Market for Corporate Control and Jobs, Majority Staff report, p. 27.
18. US Senate Investigations Committee (July 30, 2015): Impact of the U.S. Tax Code on the Market for Corporate Control and Jobs, Majority Staff report, p. 28.
19. Idem.
20. US Senate Investigations Committee (July 30, 2015): Impact of the U.S. Tax Code on the Market for Corporate Control and Jobs, Majority Staff report, p. 29.
21. Idem.

CHAPTER 12

Corporate Divestitures and Carve-Outs

12.1 General

Divestitures are major corporate restructuring transactions that narrow firm boundaries by removing one or more of a company's businesses, subsidiaries, or divisions. Divestitures happen when a company disposes of all or some of its assets by selling, exchanging, or closing them down, or through bankruptcy. As companies grow, they may decide that they are involved in too many business lines, so divestiture is the way to stay focused and remain profitable. Through divestiture, a company can eliminate redundancies, improve operational efficiency, and reduce costs. Divestiture activity reached an all-time high between 2014 and 2019, with over $1.0 trillion of transactions completed annually during this period and close to $1.5 trillion in 2015 alone.[1] A carve-out allows a company to capitalize on a business segment that may not be part of its core operations.

12.2 Reasons for Divestitures

Internal reasons that have led to divestitures include: (i) declining firm or business unit performance, (ii) unsuccessful mergers and acquisitions, (iii) over-diversification, especially when driven by empire building, and (iv) other manifestations of agency conflicts, including managerial

F. Lessambo, *U.S. Mergers and Acquisitions*,
https://doi.org/10.1007/978-3-030-85735-6_12

entrenchment or inefficient internal capital markets. Conversely divestitures can be triggered by some external factors such as: (i) include industry decline; (ii) information asymmetry vis-à-vis external constituents like securities analysts and investors; (iii) hostile takeover attempts; and (iv) regulatory requirements such as antitrust.

12.3 Voluntary vs. Involuntary Divestitures

12.3.1 Voluntary Divestitures

A voluntary divestiture may occur for several reasons, including, the shedding of poorly performing business units in order to improve overall profitability, bankruptcy avoidance, and the freeing of funds for acquisition. Sometimes, a voluntary divestiture is triggered by the fact that a previously acquired company is not integrating successfully, or an older business unit might not align with a new company strategy or the direction of new leadership. Finally, yet importantly, a thriving business may have outgrown the parent company and be ready to chart its own course with its own management and board. Changes in the market and the competitive environment, as well as the need to raise additional funds, have become key reasons for recent divestitures. Organizations in a crisis, or those that can't fix or sell an asset, should explore whether a managed exit of distressed assets can protect the remaining value.

Example: GE divests GE Capital
On April 10, 2015, parent company GE decided it would divest its GE Capital business as part of a restructuring plan. GE alleged that the divestiture of GE Capital would help the company achieve its long-term goals of growth. By the end of 2014, GE Capital's ending net investment was over $360 billion and it controlled assets worth approximately $500 billion. Thus, GE Capital was the seventh-largest bank in the U.S., a status, which makes federal regulators view GE as a Systemically Important Financial Institution. To maintain its focus on its industrial business, GE decided to divest its financial arm—GE Capital. It is worthy to recall that in the aftermath of the recession, investors were seen shying away from GE shares due to the high risk and volatility associated with GE Capital. More, when financial institutions collapsed in the recession, GE Capital was among the institutions that the federal government had to bail out in order to prevent complete failure of the banking and finance structure in the country. GE

considered that the divestiture of a majority of GE Capital will help create more value for investors and shareholders in the future. GE's industrial businesses tend to provide higher returns and with a smaller GE Capital supporting its industrial business, GE believes the company will achieve greater margins once the exit plan is complete. Nonetheless, GE hung onto some financial units used to support its remaining industrial business, such as its aircraft leasing unit and the parts of the business that finance sale of its energy and healthcare equipment.[2]

12.3.2 Involuntary Divestitures

An involuntary divestiture may occur when a merging company receives an unfavorable review by either the Federal Trade Commission or the Department of Justice, requiring it to divest a subsidiary, a business unit, or certain assets. For instance, in May 2020, the FTC Imposed conditions on AbbVie Inc.'s Acquisition of Allergan plc. The FTC requires companies to divest three drugs. After an extensive investigation, the FTC alleged that the proposed acquisition would likely result in substantial competitive harm to consumers in the market for treatment of exocrine pancreatic insufficiency, or EPI, a condition that results in the inability to digest food properly. The FTC also alleged that the acquisition would eliminate future direct competition between AbbVie and Allergan in the development and sales in the U.S. of IL-23 inhibitor drugs for treatment of moderate-to-severe Crohn's disease and moderate-to-severe ulcerative colitis. In compliance, Pharmaceutical companies AbbVie Inc. and Allergan plc have agreed to divest assets to settle Federal Trade Commission charges that AbbVie's proposed $63 billion acquisition of Allergan would violate federal antitrust law.[3] Likewise, in November 2020, the Federal Trade Commission required medical device companies Stryker Corp. and Wright Medical Group N.V. to divest all assets related to Stryker's total ankle replacements and finger joint implant products to remedy concerns that Stryker's proposed $4 billion acquisition of Wright will harm competition in those markets. The companies agreed to divest Stryker's total ankle replacements and finger joint implants businesses to DJO Global, Inc.[4]

12.4 Benefits and Drawbacks of Divestitures

12.4.1 Benefits of Divestitures

Through divestitures, firms can regain focus in their core businesses, which can lead to improvements in profitability when the focus is on operations that match the CEO's industry experience. Likewise, for firms with broad (i.e., conglomerates) divestitures can lead to improvements in profitability primarily for those firms that are able to reduce their scope and regain operational focus. Divestitures can decrease information asymmetries as well between the organization and stakeholders, or between a firm and external stakeholders. Also, divestitures allow firms to decrease the costs of managing multiple units.[5]

12.4.2 Drawbacks of Divestitures

There are direct costs involved in divestitures, including transaction and transition costs, such as the legal transfer of assets and possibly employee severance pay. It may also send a wrong signal to stakeholders. That is, if a company decides to divest itself of a business unit, but the reasons behind the move are not communicated effectively, investors may wrongly assume the divestiture is signaling the company is in financial distress.

12.5 Types of Divestitures

There are three basic types of divestitures: sell-offs spin-offs and split-ups. The choice between spin-offs, split-ups, and sell-offs is driven by several factors such as pre-divestiture market valuation of divesting firms, pre-divestiture performance of the assets being divested, and prevailing market conditions at the time of divestiture.[6]

12.5.1 Sell-Offs

In a sell-off a certain asset of the divesting firm is sold off for cash or securities to another firm or entity. A sell-off can be total or partial. In a partial sell-off, the selling company disposes of a business subsidiary to another company to raise capital and apply the funds to more productive core units instead. In a sell-off, the sale proceeds are taxable to the parent firm, which may use them for other corporate purposes or distribute to its shareholders.

- Tax treatment of assets sold

The tax law presumes that gain or loss results upon the sale or exchange of property. The character of a taxable gain or loss can be vital in determining the amount of tax due upon the sale of corporate assets. Gain can be classified as ordinary income or capital gain.

12.5.2 Spin-Offs

A spin-off is a type of divestiture in which the divested unit becomes an independent company instead of being sold to a third party. A spin-off is a transaction in which a company distributes shares in a subsidiary to the shareholders of the parent. In a full spin-off, ownership of the spun off entity is identical to ownership of the parent company immediately after the transaction. In a spin-off, a certain asset (a unit, division, or subsidiary) of a firm is split off from the parent firm into a separate publicly traded company. Shares of this new independent firm are distributed to the existing shareholders of the parent firm on a pro rata basis. In a typical 100% spin-off, all of the shares of the company being spun off are distributed to the shareholders of the parent via a dividend. This results in a full separation of the two entities in a single transaction. However, in a partial spin-off, the parent may distribute fewer than all of the shares of the spin-off company. The intent of the parent company is not to retain the remaining shares long-term, but rather to use the remaining shares in order to generate cash proceeds.[7]

- Assets and Liabilities allocation

Whether it is a 100% spin-off or a partial spin-off, the determination of the entity or segment to spin must be determined. In the case of a spin-off of a subsidiary that has been operated as a standalone business, the determination of the assets and liabilities may be simple for the business to be spun off has already been reasonably well defined. The allocation of assets and liabilities between Parent and the subsidiary to be spun (SpinCo) generally tracks the underlying businesses being retained by Parent and those being spun off with SpinCo. Therefore, assets related to, or liabilities arising from, businesses that are being spun off generally would be transferred to SpinCo.

- Structuring a Spin-off

Usually, a spin-off has no tax consequences for the divesting firm, which treats the newly created shares as a stock dividend to its existing shareholders.[8] In general, the strategy would consist of issuing new debt for the spin-off company in exchange for cash before the spin-off. Then after, distribute such cash to the parent, which the parent may then use to retire its existing debt. To retain favorable tax treatment, the parent must further transfer the proceeds of certain distributions made by the spin-off company to its parent to its shareholders or creditors. An alternative structuring strategy may consist of allowing the spin-off company to assume some of the parent's indebtedness. However, the assumption of debt may be restricted by the parent's existing debt agreements.

12.5.3 Split-Ups

A split-up refers to the action of a corporation segmenting into two or more separately run entities. A split-up is often executed either because a company seeks to slug out different business lines (i) in an effort to maximize efficiency and profitability, or (ii) because the government forces this action in an effort to combat monopolistic practices. In the former scenario, a split-up may greatly benefit shareholders, because separately managing each segment often maximizes the profits of each entity. Through synergy, the combined profits of the separated entities are expected to exceed those of the single entity from which they sprang. In the latter scenario, a split-up is compelled by antitrust laws enacted to prevent the constitution of monopolies from forming in the first place. At the completion of a split-up, the shares of the original company may be exchanged for shares in any of the new resulting entities, at the investor's discretion.

- Structuring a split-up

A split-up can be structured to be tax-free to shareholders for federal income tax purposes. In a split-up, assets are transferred from one corporation to two or more controlled corporations. The stock of the controlled corporations is then distributed to the transferor corporation's shareholders, and the transferor corporation is liquidated. The distribution of the controlled corporations' stock can be made on a pro rata or non-pro rata basis. To be tax-free the following conditions must be met: continuity-of-business-enterprise, continuity-of-shareholder-interest, and business-purpose tests.

Example: Hewlett-Packard Case
In October 2015, the Hewlett-Packard Company completed a split-up that resulted in the official formation of two new entities: HP Inc. and Hewlett-Packard Enterprises. The split-up was executed to strategically silo these two groups, because each one focused on different business models. Pointedly: Hewlett-Packard Enterprises markets hardware and software services to large businesses seeking big data storage and cloud computing technology. On the other hand, HP Inc. focuses on manufacturing personal computers, printers, and other devices geared toward small and medium-sized business owners. This split-up ultimately allowed each business entity to more efficiently run its own organizational structure, management team, salesforce, capital allocation strategy, and research and development initiatives.

After the split-up, existing shareholders of the original company and new investors alike were given the opportunity to choose which of the two new entities they wished to obtain shares in. Investors who favored exposure to a perceptively more stable, slower-growing company likely opted for shares in HP Inc., while those who preferred a faster-growing entity that could better compete in the crowded IT space likely leaned toward shares in Hewlett-Packard Enterprises.

12.6 Carve-Outs

A carve-out transaction is a deal, in which a subset of assets and liabilities are separated from, and disposed of by, a larger enterprise. It typically involves the transfer of one or more (nearly) intact business lines. Unlike the sale of a whole company, in which the buyer acquires every asset (and liability) of a going concern, the asset and liability perimeter of a carve-out transaction needs to be defined with particularity. When a carve-out is structured as a sale of assets, the buyer does not assume any liabilities that it does not contractually agree to take on.

- The Carve-Out Financial Statements

The first step in a carve-out process consists of defining the business that will be subject to the transaction and backstopping that definition with financial statements. To increase buyer confidence, the seller must provide financial, legal, and operational information that closely aligns with that business definition. More, the type of financial statements provided on the business may expand (or limit) the pool of potential buyers and the financing options available for the transaction. In small deals, buyers may get comfortable with unaudited financial statements. However, for publicly traded corporations, Rule 3-05 of Regulation S-X promulgated under the Securities Act of 1933 requires that.

- Structuring carve-out

Common structures include a direct asset sale, a sale of the entities that own transferred assets, or a mix of the two. In carve-outs structured as a straight equity sale, all contracts of the transferred entity travel with them as a matter of law when sold to the buyer. Accordingly, the contracts to which these transferred entities are party will need to be reviewed to confirm whether they include a provision that affords certain rights to the counterparty upon a change of control. In a direct asset sale structure, whenever the consent of a contractual counterparty is required before the contract can be assigned, the contract cannot be conveyed to the buyer at all until such consent is obtained. Appropriate contractual due diligence is therefore necessary to understand the interplay between the structure of the carve-out and existing commercial agreements. In considering the legal structure needed to implement the carve-out transaction, parties generally consider three key issues[9]:

i. Optimizing tax efficiency

One of the first issues to consider in structuring a carve-out transaction is the tax implications to both the buyer and the seller of any proposed structure. The most common factors include the importance to potential buyers of achieving a basis step up; the tax attributes of the parties; the existing tax liabilities; the nature of any foreign operations; and the tax consequences of any pre-transaction restructurings.

ii. Minimizing business disruption

Generally, a stock sale results in a less burdensome consent process than does an asset deal. In a stock deal, the purchaser is acquiring the stock, and all the assets and liabilities travel with the entity being acquired by operation of law. However, in an asset deal, a seller must assign each of the assets of its business.

iii. Allocating historic liabilities.

In an asset deal, only those assets and liabilities that are contractually specified are transferred. However, when the deal is structured as an asset deal, a buyer tends to assume only those liabilities arising after the closing—even if pre-closing liabilities relate to the business it is acquiring.

12.7 Divestitures Tax Considerations

From tax perspectives, divestitures are referred to as IRC Section 355 or Type D reorganization. A Type D reorganization involves a transfer of assets between corporations. ... The most common uses of D reorganizations involve the splitting of one corporation into two or more corporations in transactions commonly described as split-ups, split-offs, and spin-offs. To qualify for tax free under IRC Sect. 355 certain statutory requirements must be met: (i) control; (ii) device; (iii) active trade or business; and (iv) distribution. In addition, the transaction must satisfy certain non-statutory requirements that have developed through case law (i) business purpose; (ii) continuity of interest; and (iii) continuity of business enterprise.

12.7.1 Statutory Requirements

- Control

For purposes of IRC section 355, a corporation is considered to control another corporation if it owns stock possessing 80% of the total combined voting power of all classes of stock entitled to vote in the second corporation and at least 80% of the total number of shares of each of the other classes of stock of that corporation.

- Device

In order for section 355 to apply to the distribution of Controlled s stock, the distribution cannot be principally a device for the distribution of earnings and profits of Distributing, Controlled, or both corporations. The Treasury regulations under Sect. 355 provide certain factors that are considered evidence of a device and certain factors that are considered evidence that the transaction is not a device.

- Active trade or business

A corporation is treated as engaged in the active conduct of a trade or business if each of the following four requirements is satisfied: (i) The corporation must be currently engaged in the active conduct of a trade or business; (ii) the trade or business must have been actively conducted throughout the five-year period ending on the date of the distribution; (iii) the trade or business must not have been acquired during the five-year period ending on the date of the distribution in a transaction in which any gain or loss was recognized; and (iv) control of a corporation conducting such trade or business must not have been acquired by Distributing or any distributee corporation directly or through one or more other corporations within the five-year period preceding the distribution in a transaction in which any gain or loss was recognized.

- Distribution

Distributing must generally distribute all of the stock and securities in Controlled held by it immediately before the distribution.

12.7.2 Non-Statutory Requirements

Non-statutory requirements are requirements set up by courts. These requirements include: (i) business purpose, (ii) continuity of interest, and (iii) continuity of business enterprise.

- Business purpose

In order to qualify for the tax consequences under section 355, a valid business purpose for the transaction must also be present. The Treasury regulations incorporate this principle and specifically state that the transaction must be carried out for one or more corporate business purposes.

- Continuity of interest

IRC regulations under section 355 require that one or more persons who, directly or indirectly, were owners of the enterprise prior to the distribution or exchange own, in the aggregate, an amount of stock establishing a continuity of interest in each of the modified corporate forms in which the enterprise is conducted after the separation.

- Continuity of business enterprise

IRC section 355 contemplates the continued operation of the business or businesses existing prior to the separation. The continuity of business enterprise is deemed met whenever the prior requirements are met. That is, the IRS (The Service) would not prevent a distribution from qualifying under section 355 when the other requirements are satisfied.

Notes

1. Emilie R. Feldman (2020): Restructuring and Divestitures, The Wharton School University of Pennsylvania, p. 13.
2. Chris Isidore (2015): GE sells GE Capital unit for $26.5B, CNN Business.
3. Federal Trade Commission, May 5, 2020.
4. Federal Trade Commission, November 3, 2020.
5. Elena Vidal (2020): Divestitures, Value Creation, and Corporate Scope, pp. 6–.
6. Alexandros Prezas, Karen Simonyan (2015): Corporate divestitures: Spin-offs vs. sell-offs, Journal of Corporate Finance, Volume 34, pp. 83–107.
7. Wachtell, Lipton, Rosen & Katz (2013): Spin-Off Guide, pp. 4–5.

8. Alexandros Prezas, Karen Simonyan (2015): Corporate divestitures: Spin-offs vs. sell-offs, Journal of Corporate Finance, Volume 34, pp. 83–107.
9. Eva Davis, Kyle Gann and Rachel Ingwer (2018): *Maximizing Value & Minimizing Risks in Carve-Outs: Seller's Pre-Sale Preparation*, Winston & Strawn, LLP.

Annexes

Annex A: Acquisition Confidentiality Agreement

I/we _______________________ will receive information

concerning _______________________ (hereinafter called "the business"). As a condition I/we agree to treat any information concerning the business which is furnished to me/us in accordance with the provisions of this agreement and to take, or abstain from taking, certain actions as set out below.

1. I/we recognize and acknowledge the competitive value and confidential nature of internal, non-public financial and business information now and hereafter furnished to me/us or obtained by me/us from you or your representatives relating to the business and affairs, as well as the damage which could result to the business if any of this information is disclosed to any third party.
2. I/we hereby agree that the Material will be used solely for the purpose of the possible Acquisition, and that I/we or the directors, officers, and employees ("my/our representatives") will not disclose to any third party any of the Material now or hereafter received or provided, however, that any such information may be disclosed to my/our accountants, attorneys, and other confidential advisers who

F. Lessambo, *U.S. Mergers and Acquisitions*,
https://doi.org/10.1007/978-3-030-85735-6

need to know such information for the purpose of assisting me/us in my/our consideration of this Acquisition, who will be advised by me/us of the confidential nature of such information.

3. In addition, without the prior consent of the business owner(s) I/we will not, and nor will our representatives nor my/our advisers disclose to any person either the fact that the discussions or negotiations are taking place concerning the possible Acquisition, including the status thereof except as I/we may be required by law or any stock exchange on which my/our stocks are traded. Furthermore, no disclosure or information will be sought from any person or the staff of the business without prior authorization from the business owner(s).
4. In the event that I/we do not proceed with an offer which is the subject of this letter within a reasonable time, I/we shall promptly re-deliver to you all written Material and any other material containing or reflecting any information of the business and will not retain any copies, extracts, or other reproductions of such written material. All documents, memoranda, notes, and other writings whatsoever prepared by me/us or my/our advisers based on the information in the Material shall also be returned to you unless you agree that they may be retained, in which case they shall be kept confidential and not used by me/us or given to any third party for any purpose.
5. In the event that the possible Acquisition contemplated by this Agreement shall not be consummated, neither I/we nor my/our representatives shall use any of the non-public information now or hereafter received or obtained from the Vendor (or any related entity) with respect to any of the business or affairs of the business in furtherance of my/our business (except in negotiations of this transaction), or the business of anyone else, whether or not in competition with the business, or for any other purpose whatsoever, and I/we further agree that I/we will not solicit or entice away from the business, or any related entity, any person who was an employee of the business or any related entity at any time during the period

during which I/we receive the Material for a period of two years from the date of this Agreement.

6. All Materials furnished to me/us by you after the date hereof shall be subject to the terms of this Agreement.
7. The provisions of this letter shall be binding. I/we will procure that all of my/our subsidiary and affiliated companies comply with the provisions of this letter as if they were bound by those provisions. This letter shall be governed and construed in accordance with the laws of the state of Queensland and I/we submit to the jurisdiction of the courts exercising jurisdiction in that state.
8. I/We hereby confirm that I/we have the financial assets to acquire a business to the value of $_______________.

I/we acknowledge that by signing this agreement, I/we agree to hold all matters strictly confidential and abide by all the terms and conditions of this agreement.

I/we agree to the above (both pages 1 and 2).

_________________________ _________________________

Signature Print Name

____

Date of Signing

Please ensure that you have signed, initialed, dated, and faxed both pages.

Annex B: Mergers and Acquisitions Sample Binding Letter of Intent

Ladies and Gentlemen:

This letter agreement sets forth our agreement and understanding as to the essential terms of the sale to ________________ (the "Purchaser") by ______________ (the "Seller") of the Seller's business (the "Business"), located in _____________ and engaged in ________________. The parties intend this letter agreement to be binding and enforceable, and that it will inure to the benefit of the parties and their respective successors and assigns.

1. Purchased Assets. At the closing, the Purchaser will purchase substantially all of the assets associated with the Business, including all inventories, all intellectual property, all accounts and notes receivable, all contracts and agreements, all equipment, all legally assignable government permits, and certain documents, files and records containing technical support and other information pertaining to the operation of the Business.
2. Assumed Liabilities. The Purchaser will assume as of the closing date only those liabilities and obligations (i) arising in connection with the operation of the Business by the Purchaser after the closing date, and (ii) arising after the closing date in connection with the performance by the Purchaser of the contracts and agreements associated with the Business.
3. Purchase Price. The purchase price will be $_____, payable in cash in immediately available funds on the closing date.
4. Pre-Closing Covenants. The parties will use their reasonable best efforts to obtain all necessary third-party and government consents (including all certificates, permits, and approvals required in connection with the Purchaser's operation of the Business). The Seller will continue to operate the Business consistent with past practice. The parties agree to prepare, negotiate, and execute a purchase agreement which will reflect the terms set forth in this letter agreement, and will contain customary representations and warranties.
5. Conditions to Obligation. The Purchaser and the Seller will be obligated to consummate the acquisition of the Business unless the Purchaser has failed to obtain, despite the parties' reasonable best

efforts, all certificates, permits, and approvals that are required in connection with Purchaser's operation of the Business.

6. Due Diligence. The Seller agrees to cooperate with the Purchaser's due diligence investigation of the Business and to provide the Purchaser and its representatives with prompt and reasonable access to key employees and to books, records, contracts, and other information pertaining to the Business (the "Due Diligence Information").
7. Confidentiality; Non-competition. The Purchaser will use the Due Diligence Information solely for the purpose of the Purchaser's due diligence investigation of the Business, and unless and until the parties consummate the acquisition of the Business the Purchaser, its affiliates, directors, officers, employees, advisors, and agents (the Purchaser's "Representatives") will keep the Due Diligence Information strictly confidential. The Purchaser will disclose the Due Diligence Information only to those Representatives of the Purchaser who need to know such information for the purpose of consummating the acquisition of the Business. The Purchaser agrees to be responsible for any breach of this paragraph 7 by any of the Purchaser's Representatives. In the event the acquisition of the Business is not consummated, the Purchaser will return to the Seller any materials containing Due Diligence Information, or will certify in writing that all such materials or copies of such materials have been destroyed. The Purchaser also will not use any Due Diligence Information to compete with the Seller in the event that the acquisition of the Business is not consummated. The provisions of this paragraph 7 will survive the termination of this letter agreement.
8. Employees of the Business. Until the consummation of the acquisition of the Business, or in the event that the parties do not consummate the acquisition of the Business, the Purchaser will not solicit or recruit the employees of the Business.
9. Exclusive Dealing. Until __________, the Seller will not enter into any agreement, discussion, or negotiation with, or provide information to, or solicit, encourage, entertain or consider any inquiries or proposals from, any other corporation, fire or other person with respect to (a) the possible disposition of a material portion of the Business, or (b) any business combination involving the Business, whether by way of merger, consolidation, share exchange, or other

transaction. If for any reason the acquisition of the Business is not consummated, and the Seller is unable to enforce the provisions of this letter agreement, the Buyer will pay to the Seller a break-up fee which will equal the sum of 1% of the purchase price, and the Seller's expenses in connection with the negotiation of the acquisition.

10. Public Announcement. All press releases and public announcements relating to the acquisition of the Business will be agreed to and prepared jointly by the Seller and the Purchaser.
11. Expenses. Subject to the provisions in paragraph 9 of this letter agreement, each party will pay all of its expenses, including legal fees, incurred in connection with the acquisition of the Business.
12. Indemnification: The Seller represents and warrants that the Purchaser will not incur any liability in connection with the consummation of the acquisition of the Business to any third party with whom the Seller or its agents have had discussions regarding the disposition of the Business, and the Seller agrees to indemnify, defend, and hold harmless the Purchaser, its officers, directors, stockholders, lenders, and affiliates from any claims by or liabilities to such third parties, including any legal or other expenses incurred in connection with the defense of such claims. The covenants contained in this paragraph 12 will survive the termination of this letter agreement.

If you are in agreement with the terms of this letter agreement, please sign in the space provided below and return a signed copy to ____________________ by the close of business on ______________. Upon receipt of a signed copy of this letter, we will proceed with our plans for consummating the transaction in a timely manner.
Very truly yours,

XYZ CORPORATION
By:________________________
[Name and Title]

____

ABC CORPORATION
By: ________________________
[Name and Title]

Annex C: Term Sheet (Model Form)

[DATE] NEWCO, INC.

MEMORANDUM OF TERMS FOR PLACEMENT OF CONVERTIBLE PREFERRED

This memorandum summarizes the principal terms with respect to a private placement of equity securities of Newco (the "Company") by a group of Investors (the "Investors").

Introduction
The Company was incorporated in Delaware on [DATE]. It presently has an authorized capitalization consisting of [_____] shares of Common Stock ("Common"), [_____] shares of which have been issued to [_____] shareholders, and [_____] shares of preferred stock, [_____] shares of which have been issued to [_____] shareholders.

The Founders of the Company have purchased and paid for in full [_____] shares of the Company's Common at a price of [_____] per share. In addition there are outstanding options to purchase in the aggregate [_____] shares of Common at prices ranging from $[_____] to $[_____] per share of Common.

Proposed Private Placement
The Company and the Investors propose a private placement of shares of Preferred Stock on the following terms:

Amount
$[_____].

Type of Security
Series A Preferred Stock ("Preferred"), convertible into Common Stock representing [_____]% of the outstanding securities of the Company on a fully diluted basis.

Price Per Share
$[_____] ("Original Purchase Price").

Milestones
It is contemplated that the $[_____] Price to Investors will be available in two take-downs, the first $[_____] on the occasion of a letter of intent or interest including a comprehensive marketing plan from a major manufacturer to join in a business partnership with Newco Inc. to

market [Product] (the "Product"). The second $[_____], comprising the balance of the funds, will be advanced coincident with the execution by the Company of a formal strategic alliance with such major manufacturer.

Milestones: Rights, Preferences, Privileges, and Restrictions of Preferred Stock

1. Dividend Provisions: The holders of the Preferred will be entitled to receive dividends at the rate of $[___] per share per annum whenever funds are legally available and when and as declared by the Board. No dividend shall be paid on the Common at a rate greater than the rate at which dividends are paid on Preferred (based on the number of shares of Common into which the Preferred is convertible on the date the dividend is declared). Dividends on the Preferred will be in preference to dividends paid on the Common.

Dividends on the Preferred will be cumulative.

If dividends are cumulative, what happens upon voluntary conversion by the holder? Accumulated dividends disappear? They are paid in cash (usually without interest)? They entitle the holder to, pro tanto, more stock? What happens upon a merger in which the issuer does not survive? Upon a redemption at the option of the holder? The Company? See following discussion:

2. Liquidation Preference: In the event of any liquidation or winding up of the Company, the holders of Preferred will be entitled to receive in preference to the holders of Common an amount ("Liquidation Amount") equal to the Original Purchase Price plus any dividends declared [cumulated] on the Preferred but not paid [and then to share with the holders of the Common in the remaining assets on an as-if-converted basis]. A consolidation or merger of the Company, in which the Company does not survive, or a sale of all or substantially all of its assets shall be deemed to be a liquidation or winding up for purposes of the liquidation preference.

The language in brackets makes the preferred a participating preferred.

3. Conversion: A holder of Preferred will have the right to convert Preferred, at the option of the holder, at any time, into shares of Common. The total number of shares of Common into which Preferred may be converted initially will be determined by dividing the Original Purchase Price by the conversion price. The initial conversion price [plus the total amount of accrued but unpaid dividends] will be the Original Purchase Price. The conversion price of shares of the Preferred will be subject to proportional adjustment for stock splits, stock dividends and similar events, and to adjustment on a weighted average basis for issuances at a purchase price less than the then-effective conversion price.

The language in brackets is highly dilutive to the common, and of relatively recent original… roughly the equivalent of PIK dividends. See also the Note on Participating Preferred.

4. Automatic Conversion: Preferred will be automatically converted into Common, at the then applicable conversion price, in the event of an underwritten public offering of shares of the Common of the Company at a public offering price per share (prior to underwriter commissions and expenses) that is not less than seven times the Original Purchase Price in an offering greater than $[___] (a "Qualified IPO"). *The Preferred may be mandated to convert upon the vote of a certain percentage of the holders.*

Alternative 1: "Full Ratchet" Anti-dilution:

5. Antidilution Provisions: The conversion price of the Preferred will be subject to adjustment on a full ratchet basis to prevent dilution if the Company issues additional shares, subject to certain exceptions (including: (i) the issuance of capital stock to employees, consultants, officers or directors of the Company pursuant to stock purchase or stock option plans or agreements approved by the Board (including options granted prior to the financing), (ii) the issuance of securities in connection with acquisition or merger transactions, (iii) the issuance of securities to financial institutions or lessors in connection with commercial credit arrangements, equipment financings, or similar transactions, (iv) shares issued upon conversion of shares of Series A Preferred ("Preferred Stock"), (v) the issuance of securities in a public offering, (vi) the issuance of securities pursuant to the Warrants and currently outstanding options, warrants, notes, or other rights to acquire securities of the Company, (vii) stock splits, stock dividends or similar transactions or (viii) the issuance of the Warrants). No adjustment to the conversion price will occur for any issuance of additional shares at a purchase price in excess of the current conversion price.

"Full ratchet" anti-dilution protection was not the norm in a venture capital business until recently. It anticipates a reduction in the conversion price of a convertible preferred (and therefore an increase in the number of common shares issued to the holder upon conversion) on a dollar for dollar basis with the difference between the price per share paid, either expressly or notionally, in the so called "down round" (the dilutive round) and the

price per share and the conversion price of the convertible preferred immediately prior to the down round. Thus for example if the conversion price is currently $10 per share (which divided into the initial cost of a convertible preferred share of $100 means 10 shares of common stock issued for each share of convertible preferred traded in) and the price per share in the dilutive round is $5 then the conversion price becomes automatically $5 meaning that 20 shares will be issued versus 10 upon conversion. The reason full ratchet anti-dilution protection is viewed as unfair is it does not take into account the amount of the financing in the down round. Hypothetically, and in fact in accordance with the documents, the issuance of even one share (as against say 5,000,000 shares outstanding) at a price of $5 in the example cited would ratchet down the conversion price of all of the entire convertible preferred shares outstanding from $10 to $5. The weighted average anti-dilution provisions take into account the relative amount of the financing and therefor the perceived injury to the existing holders of convertible preferred; the full ratchet provision does not.

Alternative 2: Weighted Average Anti-dilution:
5. Anti-dilution Provisions: The conversion price of the Preferred will be subject to adjustment to prevent dilution in the event that the Company issues additional shares (other than Reserved Employee Shares) at a purchase price less than the then applicable conversion price. The conversion price will be subject to adjustment on a weighted basis, which takes into account issuances of additional shares at prices less than the applicable conversion price.

Alternative 3: "Pay-or-Play":
5. If the Company issues additional shares (other than Reserved Employee Shares) at a purchase price less than the then applicable conversion price, holders who "Participate" in such issuance will have the conversion price of their shares of Preferred adjusted on a [WEIGHTED AVERAGE or FULL RATCHET] basis.

A holder shall be deemed to decline to "Participate" in an issuance if such holder does not offer to purchase at least the same percentage of such issuance as constitutes such holder's percentage of the Conversion Shares (as determined under "Information and Registration Rights" below). If a holder declines to Participate, the Preferred held by such holder shall automatically be converted into Common at the then applicable (*i.e.* prior to the transaction) conversion price.

See Note on Pay-or-Play

6. Voting Rights: Except with respect to election of Directors, a holder of Preferred will have the right to that number of votes equal to the number of shares of Common issuable upon conversion of its Preferred. Election of Directors will be as described under "Board Representation and Meetings" below.

7. **Events of Default**: In the event of the occurrence of any of the "Events of Default" listed below, the Investors will be entitled to elect a majority of the members of the Board of Directors. "Events of Default" : shall be (i) the voluntary termination of employment of the Founder, (ii) the termination of employment of the Founder for cause, or (iii) the death or complete disability of the Founder. The rights upon the occurrence of an Event of Default will expire on a Qualified Public Offering or a merger or like reorganization in which the Company does not survive.

8. Protective Provisions: Consent of the holders of at least a majority of the Preferred will be required for any action which (i) alters or changes the rights, preferences, or privileges of the Preferred materially and adversely, (ii) increases the authorized number of shares of Preferred, (iii) creates any new class of shares having preference over or being on a parity with the Preferred, or (iv) involves sale by the Company of a substantial portion of its assets, any merger of the Company with another entity, or any amendment of the Company's articles of incorporation.

Redemption

On the fifth, sixth, and seventh anniversaries of the closing, each holder of Preferred shall be entitled to demand that one-third of the number of shares of Preferred originally purchased by such holder be redeemed by the Company, at a price equal to Original Purchase Price [plus accumulated but unpaid dividends]. To the extent that the Company may not at any such date legally redeem such Preferred, such redemption will take place as soon as legally permitted.

Information and Registration Rights

If the Company has shares outstanding with information and registration rights.

Merger of Rights: It shall be a condition of closing that the information and registration rights provisions of the agreement dated [date] between the Company and certain purchasers of the Company's stock will be merged with the registration rights of the Preferred Investors to be set forth in a Registration Rights Agreement (the "Rights Agreement") to be drafted by counsel to the Preferred Investors. All shares subject to such information and registration rights provisions shall be "Conversion Shares" as such term is used below. The Rights Agreement shall provide that:

Inconsistent voting rights in connection with multiple demand registrations is a common drafting infelicity.

Information Rights: So long as an investor holds Preferred or at least 5% of the Conversion Shares, the Company will timely furnish such investor with budgets and monthly financial statements. The obligation of the Company to furnish budgets and monthly financial statements will terminate upon a public offering of Common.

Demand Registration Rights: If, at any time after the earlier of the Company's initial public offering and the date three years from the purchase of the Preferred (but not within 6 months of the effective date of a registration), Investors holding at least 50% of the Conversion Shares request that the Company file a Registration Statement for at least 20% of the Conversion Shares (or any lesser percentage if the anticipated aggregate offering price, net of underwriting discounts and commissions would exceed $[_____]), the Company will use its best efforts to cause such shares to be registered. The Company will not be obligated to effect more than three registrations (other than on Form S-3) under these demand right provisions.

Registrations on Form S-3: Holders of at least 25% of the Conversion Shares will have the right to require the Company to file an unlimited number of Registration Statements on Form S-3 (or any equivalent successor form).

Piggyback Registration: The holders of the Conversion Shares will be entitled to "piggyback" registration rights on registrations of the Company, subject to the right of the Company and its underwriters, in view of market conditions, to reduce the number of shares of the Investors proposed to be registered.

Registration Expenses: The registration expenses (exclusive of underwriting discounts and special counsel fees of a selling shareholder) of three demand registrations and three piggybacks will be borne by the

Company, and all other expenses of registered offerings shall be borne pro rata among the selling shareholders and, if it participates, the Company.

Transfer of Registration Rights: The registration rights may be transferred to a transferee (other than a competitor of the Company) who acquires at least 20% of the shares held by a holder of Conversion Shares. Transfer of registration rights to a partner of any investor will be without restriction as to minimum shareholding.

Future Purchasers: Subsequent purchasers of the Company's securities to whom the Company grants information and registration rights shall become parties to the Rights Agreement upon consent of the holders of 66 2/3% of the Conversion Shares.

Other Registration Provisions: Other provisions will be contained in the Purchase Agreement with respect to registration rights as are reasonable, including cross-indemnification, the Company's ability to delay the filing of the demand registration for a period of not more than 120 days, the agreement by Preferred holders if requested by the underwriter in a public offering not to sell any unregistered Conversion Shares they hold for a period of up to 120 days following the effective date of the Registration Statement of such offering, the period of time during which the Registration Statement will be kept effective, underwriting arrangements and the like. The registration rights will only apply to Common issued upon conversion of Preferred and the Company shall have no obligation to register an offering of Preferred.

Board Representation and Company Meetings

The corporate documents of the Company will provide that the authorized number of directors will be [_____]. So long as 25% or more of the Preferred issued in the financing remain outstanding, the Preferred (voting as a class) will elect [_____] directors, the Common (voting as a class) will elect [_____] directors, and the remaining [_____] directors will be elected by both the Common and the Preferred, each voting together as one class. If at any time, less than 25% of the Preferred remains outstanding, all of the directors will be elected by the Preferred and Common voting together as one class, and the Preferred will be entitled to vote as if all of the Preferred were converted to Common. The Board will meet at least quarterly. The bylaws will provide that any two directors or holders of at least 25% of the Preferred may call a meeting of the Board of Directors. In case of an Event of Default, the rights of the Preferred to elect a majority of the board will be as stated above.

Employment Agreements; New Hire
The Company has or will have employment agreements with the following persons: [NAMES]. The Company will elect persons acceptable to the Investors to the following positions:

[POSITIONS]

Employee Shares; Benchmarks
If the Company meets certain benchmarks (set forth below), the Compensation Committee of the Company's Board of Directors shall grant incentive stock options to purchase a number of shares (the "Employee Shares") of Common Stock of the Company to the Founder (the "Founder") and the Company's employees which will result in the Founder and such employees owning [________]% of the Company's outstanding capital stock after the Third Round Financing (as defined below). The Founder and Co-Founder shall receive shares which will result in each owning [________]% and [______]% of such capital stock, respectively, and will be granted options to acquire shares equal in number to [[______]% of such percentages at Closing. Such "early" options will only become exercisable, however, if the benchmarks set forth below are met. None of the remaining options shall be granted to the Founder, Co-Founder, or other employees until closing of the Third Round Financing and will be granted at an exercise price equal to the fair market value of the Common Stock at that time. Shares acquired by the Founder and Co-Founder upon their exercise of the "early" options shall vest for three years from closing of the Third Round Financing minus the amount of time each has been employed by the Company.

Benchmarks: For the Employee Shares to become exercisable or to be granted the following benchmarks must be met:

1. Second Round Financing
    1. Price of $0.50 per share
    2. Proceeds of $[____]
    3. New investor participates
    4. Closes within 9 months of First Round Financing
2. Third Round Financing
    1. Price of $0.00 per share

2. Proceeds of $[____]
3. New investor participates
4. Closes within 12 months of Second Round Financing

If the Company shall not satisfy the Second Round Financing benchmarks but shall satisfy the Third Round Financing benchmarks, then the number of Employee Shares issued shall be reduced from shares resulting in ownership of [____]% to [____]%. The Compensation Committee shall meet every six months to reevaluate the criteria set forth above and may, in its sole discretion, alter it. However, the Committee may not change the benchmarks so that they become more difficult for the Company to meet.

Compensation Committee
The Board of Directors shall appoint a Compensation Committee consisting of the two representatives of the Preferred and the Independent Director which shall be responsible for administering the benchmarks, granting the Employee Shares, and compensation of all officers of the Company. Until the closing of the Second Round Financing, the Preferred shall only have one representative serving on the Committee.

Key-Person Insurance
It shall be a condition of the closing that the Company obtain $[___] of key-person insurance on each of.

[NAMES].

Stock Restriction Agreements
The Founders and all other holders of Common of the Company who are employees of, or consultants to, the Company will execute a Stock Restriction Agreement with the Company pursuant to which the Company will have a repurchase option to buy back at cost a portion of the shares of Common Stock held by such person in the event that such shareholder's employment with, or consulting to, the Company is terminated prior to the expiration of 48 months from the date of the purchase of the Preferred or date of first employment or consulting, whichever is later (the "Measuring Date"). A portion of the shares will be released from the repurchase option based upon continued employment by the Company as follows: 25% will be released from the repurchase option at the end of 12 months from the Measuring Date, 25% will be released at the end of 24 months from the Measuring Date and thereafter 1/24th

of the remaining shares will be released from the repurchase option per month. In addition, the Company will have a right of first refusal with respect to any employee's or consultant's shares proposed to be resold. The price at which the Company may exercise its right of first refusal will be equal to the lower of (i) the price offered by the proposed third party purchaser and (ii) the price most recently set by the Board of Directors as the fair market value of the Common. The right of first refusal will terminate upon a qualified IPO.

***Note On Reverse Vesting**: Reverse vesting is often taken to be an aggressive and abusive tactic by venture capitalists to assert control over the founder, entrepreneur and other employees who, prior to the round in question, enjoyed vesting shares... a method of turning the founder into an employee and giving the VCs the opportunity to treat him/her accordingly. However, there are perfectly sound economics behind reverse vesting, the same economics behind vesting in the first instance, and the same involved in the question of accelerated vesting on changes of control. The ultimate rewards of the key managers, their equity positions, are subject to vesting, and the ownership interests of the other equity holders are more valuable. The New York Yankees, for example, are a much more valuable franchise if the key players are signed to long-term contracts and cannot take the money and run, so to speak. Reverse vesting does have a control aspect to it; but often the VCs are in control in any event. The more significant imperative behind reverse vesting is economic. The VCs in the round are attempting to improve the enterprise value of the company allocated to their shares.*

Restrictions on Transfer

The present holders of the Company's common will agree to restrictions on transfer (with customary exceptions) in favor of the Company and/or the Series A Preferred in the event of any voluntary or involuntary transfer.

Market Standoff Agreement

It will be a condition of closing that the Company will cause all present holders of the Company's Common and all present holders of options to purchase, or rights to convert into, the Company's Common to execute a Market Standoff Agreement with the Company pursuant to which such holders will agree, if so requested by the Company or any underwriter's representative in connection with the first two public offerings of the Company's Common, not to sell or otherwise transfer any securities of the Company during a period of up to 120 days following the effective date of the applicable registration statements. The Company will covenant that all future purchasers of stock prior to the Company's initial public offering will execute such a Market Standoff Agreement.

Reserved Employee Shares

The Company may reserve up to [____] shares of its Common (the "Reserved Employee Shares") including shares presently reserved for issuance upon the exercise of outstanding options for issuance to Employees.

The Reserved Employee Shares will be issued from time to time under such arrangements, contracts or plans as are recommended by management and approved by the Board. Issuance of shares to employees in excess of the Reserved Employee Shares will be dilutive events requiring adjustment of the conversion price as provided above and will be subject to the Investors' right of first refusal described below. Holders of Reserved Employee Shares will be required to execute Stock Restriction Agreements as described above.

Preemptive Right

If the Company offers equity securities (other than Reserved Employee Shares, or in connection with an acquisition of technology or a business), each holder of Preferred [and each Founder] will be entitled to purchase the same percentage of such offering as such holder purchased of the shares of Preferred issued in this private placement. This right will terminate upon an initial public offering.

Right of Co-Sale

If any Founder proposes to sell his shares of the Company, each holder of Preferred will be entitled to participate in such sale by selling the same percentage of his Preferred as such Founder is selling of such Founder's Common. This right will terminate upon the Company's initial public offering.

Sale of the Company (Drag Along Rights)

If an unaffiliated third party makes a bona fide offer for all the stock or substantially all the assets of the Company (or to lease its product line on an exclusive basis) and the holders of the Preferred elect to sell, the Founders shall have 30 days to match the offer and, failing their ability to do so (with financing in place), they shall sell their shares or vote to sell assets or lease product to other third party on the same terms.

There are several issues, as yet untested, as drag-along rights, the preferred and common are likely to be offered different prices. Can the preferred force a drag-along if the common shareholders object to the price difference? Forum Discussion.

Proprietary Information and Inventions Agreement
Each officer, director and key employee of the Company will enter into a proprietary information and inventions agreement in a form reasonably acceptable to the Company and the Investors.

Negative Covenants
So long as 10 percent or more of the shares of Series B Preferred remain outstanding, without the approval of a majority in interest of the holders, the Company will not take any action that: (i) Alters or changes the rights, preferences or privileges of the shares of Series A Preferred materially and adversely, (ii) increases or decreases the number of authorized shares of Series B Preferred (it being acknowledged that a sufficient number of shares shall be authorized to permit the Company to convert the Class A and Class B Mandatory Convertible Promissory Notes and to raise additional funds to close the financing at $10,000,000), (iii) authorizes the issuance of securities having a preference over or on a par with the shares of Series A Preferred, (iv) amends the Company's Certificate of Incorporation such that the holders of the Series A.

Preferred are affected materially and adversely, (v) amend the Company's By-Laws such that the holders of the Series A Preferred are affected materially and adversely, (vi) authorize a merger, consolidation, reorganization or sale of the Company or substantially all of its assets, (vii) change the size of the Board.

Warrants
The holders of Series A Preferred shall be granted warrants (the "Warrants") to purchase additional shares of Common Stock equal to (i) [50%] multiplied by (ii) the number of shares of Series A Preferred, they owned as of the closing. The Warrants shall have an exercise price equal to [$.50] per share and shall be exercisable for the [$.50] per share for the three year period following the closing.

The Purchase Agreement
The purchase of the Preferred will be made pursuant to a Stock Purchase Agreement drafted by counsel to the Investors and reasonably acceptable to the Company and the Investors. The Purchase Agreement will contain,

among other things, appropriate representations and warranties of the Company, covenants of the Company reflecting the provisions set forth herein, and appropriate conditions including qualification of the shares under applicable Blue Sky laws, the filing of a Certificate of Amendment to the Company's Articles of Incorporation to authorize the Preferred, and opinions of counsel.

One should be aware that some of the typical provisions found in a term sheet, i.e., "customary representations and warranties," can constitute less than precise instructions to the draftsmen of the Stock Purchase Agreement.

Expenses

The Company and the Investors will each bear their own legal and other expenses with respect to the transaction (except that, assuming a successful completion of the offering, the Company will pay at the Closing the reasonable legal fees incurred by a single counsel to all Investors).

Finders

The Company and the Investors will each indemnify the other for any finder's fees for which either is responsible.

No Shop, No Solicit

Cross-reference Note on 'No Shop, No Solicitation' Clauses.

Newco, Inc. a Delaware corporation ("Newco"), and XYZ Partners, LP (herein the "Fund"), are currently involved in negotiations with respect to an investment by the Fund in Newco's equity securities.

The Company recognizes that the Investors have and will expend considerable resources and executive time in negotiating a definitive agreement with respect to the investments (herein the "Investment," which term includes, as the context may allow or require, any acquisition of Newco securities or assets by way of a merger, sale of assets, consolidation or like transaction, by the Fund in Newco and performing its due diligence review of Newco. Accordingly, following the execution of this Term Sheet, Newco and its shareholders, directors, members, employees, financial advisors, brokers, stockholders or any person acting on their or its behalf (the "Principals"), shall immediately halt any discussions with other potential Investor in (including persons interested in an Acquisition) Newco (including persons with whom Newco or its.

Principals may have had discussions prior to the date hereof), except to advise such person that a prospective Investor has been granted the exclusive right to negotiate concerning a proposed Investment (without identifying the Fund) and that Newco and its Principals are legally bound to a "quiet period" covering any Investment transaction. Without limiting the generality of the foregoing, Newco and/or its Principals will not hold any discussions with, or provide any information to, any person, or respond to any inquiry made by any person, concerning a proposed Investment or cooperate in any way with, or assist or participate in, facilitate or encourage, any effort or attempt by any third party to do or seek any of the foregoing.

The Fund, Newco and the Principals hereby agree to proceed in good faith toward negotiation and execution as soon as possible after the date hereof of the definitive documents [based on the Term Sheet] related to the consummation of the Investment, including the stock purchase agreement and any additional agreements deemed necessary or advisable by the parties (the "Investment Documents") that will contain mutually agreeable terms, representations, conditions, covenants and indemnities.

If at any time prior to [date] (the "Expiration Date") Newco is approached by any third party concerning participation in a transaction involving its assets or business, or securities issued or to be issued by Newco, then Newco shall promptly inform the Investors of the nature of such contact and the parties thereto, and shall furnish the Investors a copy of any inquiry or proposal, or, if not in writing, a description thereof, including the name of the counterparty or parties (any such person, together with all other third parties referred to in this and the preceding paragraphs, being referred to herein as a "Competing Person").

It is understood and agreed that money damages would not be a sufficient remedy for any breach of this Section by Newco or any of its Principals and that the Fund shall be entitled to seek equitable relief, including injunction and specific performance, as a remedy for any such breach. Such remedies shall not be deemed to be the exclusive remedies for a breach of this letter agreement but shall be in addition to all other remedies available at law or equity. Without limiting the generality of the foregoing, in the event of breach of the provisions hereof by Newco and/or any of its Principals, accompanied by an investment in Newco securities by a Competing Person at any time within 24 months following the Expiration Date, Newco will issue to the Fund a five (5) year transferable warrant to purchase shares of Newco common stock equal to [2%] of Newco's common stock (on a fully diluted basis, following the Investment by the Competing Person), the exercise price of such warrant to be equal to the price per share described in Section 3.

Closing
The closing of the transaction is expected to occur on or before [DATE].

Nonbinding Character
The parties expressly agree that, except with respect to the provisions of paragraphs 28, 29, 30 and 31, no binding obligations will be created until a document entitled "final agreement of purchase and sale" is executed with the requisite formality and delivered by both parties. Without limiting the generality of the foregoing, it is the parties' intent that, until that event, no agreement shall exist between them and that there be no obligations whatsoever based on such as parole evidence, extended negotiations, "handshakes," oral understanding, or courses of conduct (including reliance and changes of position). No legally binding obligations whatsoever are to be created, implied, or inferred, until a document explicitly entitled "final" has been executed and delivered.

In addition, neither party is under any obligation to negotiate in good faith or to use any quantum of effort, including but not limited to "best efforts," to reach an agreement. Either party is free to negotiate with a third party at the same time it is negotiating with the other party to this document and, except as explicitly.

herein provided, to solicit interest from any available source. Either party may reveal information, whether labeled "confidential" or otherwise, obtained in the course of the transaction unless there is a specific agreement, signed by both parties with the requisite formality, to keep a particular item of information confidential.

Annex D: Engagement Letter

CONFIDENTIAL

July 20th, 2020.
Ms. Penelope Richards
Chairman, President & Chief Executive Officer
East London Savings Bank
145 Bishop Street
New England, MA 02,128
RE: Acquisition Advisory Services

Dear Ms. Richards:
This agreement sets forth the terms and conditions under which East London Savings Bank ("Company") has engaged the services of Joni Mueller & Co., Inc., ("JMCO") to act as its financial advisor in connection with the potential acquisition of the institutions identified in the Schedule attached hereto (the "Targets").

1. Services

A. JMCO will provide the following merger and acquisition related services to the Company:

(i) JMCO will review and analyze, using several analytical models, such financial market and other data, as necessary, to express an opinion on the value of the Target;

(ii) JMCO will help formulate and recommend an exchange ratio(s) or (if other than a stock-for-stock exchange) alternative transaction structures to accomplish the proposed acquisition of Target. Any definitive agreement entered into by the Company involving the sale, merger or other business combination involving at least 80% of the Target's stock or assets shall be a "Transaction";

(iii) JMCO will recommend the form and structure of the proposed acquisition with specific reference to the accounting and tax consequences to each party from a corporate point of view;

(iv) The conclusions, opinions and recommendations resulting from the above will be presented to the management and Board of the Company;

(v) JMCO will be available for discussion of results and the recommended structure and acquisition price as requested and will negotiate with Target's representatives toward reaching an agreement for a possible acquisition;

(vi) JMCO will conduct a due diligence investigation on Target. JMCO understands that the Company intends to conduct comprehensive due diligence;

(vii) JMCO will, if requested by the Company, issue a separate written opinion as to the fairness from a financial point of view, to the Directors and/or shareholders of the Company, depending upon the transaction structure, of either the Exchange Ratio or the consideration ("Consideration") to be paid by the Company ("Opinion"). The Company may reproduce the Opinion in full in any disclosure document or proxy statement relating to such Transaction (the "Statement") that the Company files under the Securities Exchange Act of 1934 or any other federal or state law and distributes to its shareholders; in such event, the Company may also include references to the Opinion and to JMCO and its relationship with the Company in the Statement. Any references to JMCO in the Statement shall be approved by JMCO; and

(viii) JMCO will review all agreements, regulatory applications, filings and shareholders communications in connection with the proposed acquisition and provide comments where needed. JMCO will also be available to meet with the various regulatory authorities to review the details of the Transaction.

B. Advisory and Other Fee

For all the services rendered hereunder, (including without limitation rendering the fairness opinion) JMCO shall be entitled to a financial advisory fee (the "Contingent Advisory Fee") as established on the attached Schedule. Thirty-five percent (35%) of the amount of the Contingent Advisory Fee shall be due and payable upon execution of a definitive acquisition agreement with respect to the Transaction and the remainder shall be due and payable upon closing of the Transaction.

In addition to the Contingent Advisory Fee payable to JMCO under this Agreement, the Company agrees to reimburse JMCO upon request for its out-of-pocket expenses incurred in connection with its services under this Agreement whether or not the Transaction is consummated, including the fees and disbursements of RBCO's legal counsel (the "Expense Reimbursement"). JMCO's general out-of-pocket and legal expenses will be billed to the Company quarterly and be payable as submitted. Such expenses shall not exceed $15,000 without the prior consent of the Company.

2. Other Advisory Services and Offerings

The Company also appoints JMCO to act in the following capacities in any of the following transactions entered into or contemplated by the Company (each, an "Other Transaction"), which is necessary for or contemplated by a Transaction.

i. **Capital Raising**: Lead manager, underwriter or placement agent and financial advisor in connection with any offering of equity or other capital markets financing.

JMCO's appointment with respect to an Other Transaction shall be for the term of this Engagement Letter. JMCO's compensation in connection with any Other Transaction shall be determined by agreement between the Company and JMCO on the basis of compensation customarily paid to financial advisors, underwriters or placement agents in similar transactions.

3. Information to be Supplied; Confidentiality

(a) In connection with JMCO's activities on behalf of the Company, the Company will furnish JMCO with all financial and other information regarding the Company that JMCO reasonably believes appropriate to its assignment (all such information so furnished by the Company, whether furnished before or after the date of this Agreement, being referred to herein as the "Information"). The Company will provide JMCO with access to the officers, directors, employees, independent accountants, legal counsel and other advisors and consultants for the Company. The Company recognizes and agrees that JMCO:

i. will use and rely primarily on the Information and information available from generally recognized public sources in performing the services contemplated by this Agreement without independently verifying the information or such other information;

ii. does not assume responsibility for the accuracy of the Information or such other information; and

iii. will not make an appraisal of any assets or liabilities owned or controlled by the Company or its market competitors.

(b) JMCO will maintain the confidentiality of the Information and, unless and until such information shall have been made publicly available by the Company or by others without breach of a confidentiality agreement, shall disclose the Information only as authorized by the Company or as required by law or by order of a governmental authority or court of competent jurisdiction. In the event that JMCO is legally required to make disclosure of any of the Information, JMCO will give notice to the Company prior to such disclosure, to the extent that JMCO can practically do so.

The foregoing paragraph shall not apply to information that:

i. at the time of disclosure by the Company is, or thereafter becomes, generally available to the public or within the industries in which the Company or JMCO or its affiliates conduct business, other than as a direct result of a breach by JMCO of its obligations under this Agreement;

ii. prior to or at the time of disclosure by the Company, was already in the possession of, or conceived by, JMCO or any of its affiliates, or could have been developed by them from information then in their possession, by the application of other information or techniques in their possession, generally available to the public, or available to JMCO or its affiliates other than from the Company;

iii. at the time of disclosure by the Company or thereafter, is obtained by JMCO or any of its affiliates from a third party who JMCO reasonably believes to be in possession of the information not in violation of any contractual, legal or fiduciary obligation to the Company with respect to that information; or

iv. is independently developed by JMCO or its affiliates.

(c) Nothing in this Agreement shall be construed to limit the ability of JMCO or its affiliates to pursue, investigate, analyze, invest in, or engage in investment banking, financial advisory or any other business relationships with entities other than the Company, notwithstanding that such entities may be engaged in a business which is similar to or competitive with the business of the Company, and notwithstanding that such entities may have actual or potential operations, products, services, plans, ideas, customers or supplies similar or identical to the Company's, or may have been identified by the Company as potential merger or acquisition targets or potential candidates for some other business combination, cooperation or relationship. JMCO represents that it is not presently representing any of the entities listed on the Schedule, and will not do so with respect to those entities now or subsequently listed, without advance notice to Company. The Company expressly acknowledges and agrees that it does not claim any proprietary interest in the identity of any other entity in its industry or otherwise, and that the identity of any such entity is not confidential information.

(d) The Company acknowledges that all advice (written or oral) given by JMCO to the Company is intended solely for the benefit and use of the Company. Other than to the extent required to be reflected in Board and committee meeting minutes, no advice (written or oral) of JMCO hereunder shall be used, reproduced, disseminated, quoted or referred to at any time, in any manner, or for any purpose, nor shall any public references to JMCO be made by the Company (or such persons), without the prior written consent of JMCO.

4. Indemnification, Contribution and Limitation of Liability

The Company agrees to indemnify JMCO and its controlling persons, representatives and agents in accordance with the indemnification provisions set forth in Appendix I, and agrees to the other provisions of Appendix I, which is incorporated herein by this reference, regardless of whether the proposed Transaction is consummated.

5. Term of Engagement Period; Survival of Provisions

(a) The term of JMCO's engagement with respect to the Transaction (the "Engagement Period") shall be for one year commencing on the date of execution of this Agreement or, if earlier, upon written notice by either party to the other; provided, however, in any event that if the Company is negotiating a Transaction at the completion of the Engagement Period or is awaiting regulatory approval of a Transaction entered into during the term of the Engagement Period, then the Engagement Period is automatically extended until the contemplated Transaction is consummated or terminated. JMCO will be entitled to its full fee under Sect. 1 herein in the event that at any time prior to the expiration of one year after termination of the Engagement Period a Transaction is consummated with any of the potential Targets with which JMCO has had discussions and which are identified by JMCO to the Company on the Schedule or added to the Schedule subsequently by mutual agreement.

(b) This Agreement and the Appendices shall survive any termination of the Engagement Period.

(c) During the Engagement Period, the Company will not solicit or negotiate with any other person to act as financial advisor, underwriter, or placement agent or to provide other investment banking services to the Company with respect to those entities identified on the Schedule.

6. Independent Contractor: No Fiduciary Duty

The Company acknowledges and agrees that it is a sophisticated business enterprise and that JMCO has been retained pursuant to this Agreement to act as financial advisor to the Company solely with respect to the matters set forth herein. In such capacity, JMCO shall act as an independent contractor, and any duties of JMCO arising out of its engagement pursuant to this Agreement shall be contractual in nature and shall be owed solely to the Company. Each party disclaims any intention to impose any fiduciary duty on the other.

7. Beneficiaries

This Agreement shall inure to the sole and exclusive benefit of JMCO and the Company and the persons referred to in Appendix I and their respective successors and representatives. The obligations and liabilities under this Agreement shall be binding upon JMCO and the Company.

8. Governing Law

This Agreement shall be governed by and construed in accordance with the laws of the State of New York applicable to contracts executed and to be wholly performed therein without giving effects to its conflicts of laws principles or rules. Any dispute hereunder shall be brought in a court in the State of New York.

9. Amendments

This Agreement may be modified or amended, or its provisions waived, only by an instrument in writing signed by the person or persons against whom enforcement of this modification, amendment or waiver is sought.

10. Announcements of Offering and Other Transactions

If the Transaction or Other Transaction is consummated in which JMCO acts as financial advisor or otherwise, JMCO may, at its option and expense, place an announcement in such newspapers and periodicals as JMCO may choose stating that RBCO has so acted, and the capacity in which it has acted.

11. No Commitment

This Agreement does not ensure the successful arrangement or completion of the Transaction or any Other Transaction.

12. Entire Agreement

This Agreement constitutes the entire Agreement between the parties and supersedes and cancels any and all prior or contemporaneous arrangements, understandings and agreements, written or oral, between them relating to the subject matter hereof.

13. Severability

If any portion of this Agreement shall be held or made unenforceable or invalid by a statute, rule, regulation, decision of a tribunal or otherwise, the remainder of this Agreement shall not be affected thereby and shall remain in full force and effect, and, to the fullest extent, the provisions of the Agreement shall be severable.

14. Headings

The descriptive headings of the paragraphs, subparagraphs and Appendices of this Agreement are inserted for convenience only and do not constitute a part of this Agreement and shall not affect in any way the meaning or interpretations of this Agreement.

15. Failure or Delay; No Waiver

It is understood and agreed that failure or delay by either the Company or JMCO in exercising any right, power or privilege hereunder shall not operate as a waiver thereof, nor shall any single or partial exercise thereof preclude any other or further exercise thereof or the exercise of any other right, power, or privilege hereunder.

16. Waiver of Trial by Jury

EACH OF RBCO AND THE COMPANY WAIVES ALL RIGHT TO TRIAL BY JURY IN ANY ACTION, PROCEEDING, CLAIM OR COUNTERCLAIM (WHETHER BASED ON CONTRACT, TORT OR OTHERWISE) RELATED TO OR ARISING OUT OF THIS AGREEMENT.

If the foregoing terms correctly set forth our agreement, please sign and return to us a duplicate copy of this Agreement. We look forward to working with you toward the successful conclusion of this engagement and developing a long term relationship with the Company.

Very truly yours,

	Confirmed and accepted as of this _____ day of______, 2020
JONI MUELLER & CO., INC	**EAST LONDON SAVINGS BANK**
By:____________________	By:________________________
Patrick Pearl Chairman & CEO	Penelope Richards Chairman, President & CEO

Appendix I

This Appendix I is attached to and incorporated by reference into the engagement letter, dated January 9, 2003 ("Engagement Letter"), between Joni Mueller & Co., Inc. ("JMCO") and East London Savings Bank (the "Company").

In the event that JMCO becomes involved in any capacity in any action, proceeding or investigation brought by or against any person (including an action or proceeding brought by a shareholder of the Company), in connection with or as a result of either our engagement or any matter referred to in our Engagement Letter, the Company periodically on demand will reimburse JMCO for its reasonable legal and other expenses (including the reasonable cost to JMCO of any investigation and preparation and including the reasonable appropriate hourly charges of JMCO's officers and employees) incurred in connection therewith; provided, however, that if in any such action, proceeding or investigation it is found by a court in a final judgment that any loss, claim, damage or liability of JMCO has resulted from the gross negligence or willful misconduct of JMCO in performing the services which were the subject of the Engagement Letter, JMCO shall repay such portion of the reimbursed amounts that is attributable to expenses incurred in relation to the act or omission of JMCO which is the subject of such finding. The Company also will indemnify and hold JMCO harmless against any and all losses, claims, damages or liabilities to any such person in connection with or as a result of either JMCO's engagement by the Company or any matter referred to in the Engagement Letter, except to the extent that in any such action, proceeding or investigation it is found by a court in a final judgment that any such loss, claim, damage or liability has resulted from the gross negligence or willful misconduct of JMCO in performing the services which were the subject of the Engagement Letter. If for any reason the foregoing indemnification is unavailable to RBCO or insufficient to hold it harmless, then the Company shall contribute to the amount paid or payable by JMCO as a result of such loss, claim, damage or liability in such proportion as is appropriate to reflect the relative benefits received by the Company and its shareholders on the one hand and JMCO on the other hand in the matters contemplated by the Engagement Letter as well as the relative fault of the Company and JMCO with respect to such loss, claim, damage or liability and other relevant equitable considerations; provided however, that JMCO shall not be obligated to contribute any amount hereunder that exceeds the amount of the compensation paid to JMCO hereunder. The reimbursement, indemnity and contribution obligations of the Company under this paragraph shall be in addition to any liability which the Company may otherwise have, shall extend upon the same terms and conditions to any affiliate of JMCO and the directors, officers, employees, agents and controlling persons (if any) of JMCO and similarly to the directors, officers, employees, agents and controlling persons (if any) of any such affiliate, and shall be binding upon and inure to the benefit of any successors, assigns, heirs and personal representatives of the Company, JMCO, any such affiliate and any such person. The Company also agrees that neither JMCO nor any of such affiliates, directors, officers, employees, agents or controlling persons shall have any liability to the Company or any person asserting claims on behalf of or in right of the Company in connection with or as a result of either our engagement or any matter referred to in this letter except to the extent that any losses, claims, damages, liabilities or expenses incurred by the Company are found by a court in a final judgment to have resulted from the gross negligence or willful misconduct of JMCO in performing the services that are the subject of this letter. The provisions of this paragraph shall survive any termination or completion of the engagement provided by the Engagement Letter.

EXHIBIT 1.1

CONFIDENTIAL

July 9, 2020
Ms. Penelope Richards
Chairman, President & Chief Executive Officer
East London Savings Bank
145 Bishop Street
New England, MA 0218

Re: Mutual to Stock Conversion—Subscription Enhancement & Administrative Services.

Dear Ms. Richards:

Joni Mueller & Co., Inc. ("JMCO") is pleased to submit this engagement letter setting forth the terms of the proposed engagement between JMCO and East London Savings Bank, (the "Institution") in connection with the potential corporate reorganization of the Institution and sale of common stock by the Institution.

1. BACKGROUND ON JONI MUELLER

Joni Mueller & Co., Inc. was organized in 2001 and is one of the nation's leading investment bankers for financial institutions. The firm is a registered broker-dealer with the Securities and Exchange Commission, a member of the National Association of Securities Dealers, Inc., Securities Industry Association and a member of the Securities Investor Protection Corporation. JMCO's Financial Institutions Group represents one of the largest such groups devoted solely to financial institution matters in the country.

2. MUTUAL TO STOCK CONVERSION AND STOCK OFFERING

It is our understanding that the Institution is considering the acquisition of another depository institution as identified in the Schedule attached hereto (a "Transaction") and in connection therewith the potential (1) reorganization into a two-tier mutual holding company structure by forming a mutual holding company and middle-tier holding company ("Holding Company") pursuant to applicable regulations; or (2) reorganization into a fully converted public company. In each case common stock (the "Common Stock") would be offered in a subscription offering with any remaining shares sold in a community offering (collectively the

"Offering"). In connection therewith, the Institution's Board of Directors would adopt a stock issuance plan (the "Plan") whereby shares of Common Stock would be offered for sale in the Offering. In connection with the Offering, JMCO would propose to act as financial advisor to the Institution with respect to the Plan and selling agent/manager with respect to the Offering of the shares of Common Stock in the Offering. Specific terms of services shall be set forth in a definitive agency agreement (the "Definitive Agreement") between JMCO and the Institution to be executed on the date the offering document is declared effective by the appropriate regulatory authorities.

Although this engagement letter applies only to a conversion and Offering in connection with a Transaction, the Institution expects that during the term of this engagement letter it will consult with JMCO, prior to engaging in any conversion and Offering, about involving JMCO in that conversion and Offering, and would execute another engagement letter if the parties agree on the terms of such involvement.

3. SERVICES To BE PROVIDED BY JONI MUELLER

a. Advisory Services—Thorough planning is essential to a successful offering. JMCO serves as lead coordinator of the financial advisory, marketing and logistic efforts necessary to prepare for an offering. Our actions are intended to clearly define responsibilities and timetables, while avoiding costly surprises. We assume responsibility for the initial preparation of marketing materials—saving you time and legal expense. Moreover, as your investment banker, JMCO, will evaluate the financial, marketing and regulatory issues involved in the Offering. Our specific responsibilities include:

- Advise with respect to business planning issues in preparation for a public offering;
- Advise with respect to the choice of charter and form of organization;
- Review and advise with respect to the Plan;
- Review and provide input with respect to the Business Plan to be prepared in connection with the Offering;
- Participate in drafting the Prospectus and assist in obtaining all requisite regulatory approvals;
- Review and provide to the Board of Directors on the adequacy of the appraisal process;

- Develop a marketing plan for the Offering including direct mail, advertising, community meetings and telephone solicitation;
- Provide specifications and assistance in selecting data processing assistance, printer and other professionals;
- Develop an operating plan for the Stock Sale Center (the "Center");
- Provide a list of equipment and supplies needed for the Center;
- Draft marketing materials including letters, brochures, slide show script and advertisements; and
- Assist in arranging market-makers for post-reorganization trading.

b. Administrative Services and Stock Sale Center Management—JMCO will manage all aspects of the Offering. A successful Offering requires an enormous amount of attention to detail. Working knowledge and familiarity with the law and "lore" of bank regulators, Securities and Exchange Commission and NASD is essential. JMCO's experience in managing many thrift reorganizations and mutual holding company minority stock offerings will minimize the burden on your management and disruption to normal banking business. At the same time, our legal, accounting and regulatory background ensures that details are attended to in a professional fashion. An Offering requires accurate and timely record keeping and reporting. Furthermore, customer inquiries must be handled professionally and accurately. The Center centralizes all data and work effort relating to the Offering.

JMCO will supervise and administer the Center. We will train Center staff to help record stock orders, answer customer inquiries and handle special situations as they arise. Center activities include the following:

- Provide experienced on-site registered representatives to minimize disruption of day-to-day business;
- Identify and organize space for the Center, the focal point of sales and proxy solicitation activity;
- Administer the Center. All substantive stock and proxy related matters will be handled by employees of JMCO;
- Organize and implement all proxy solicitation efforts (if applicable);

- Prepare procedures for processing proxies, stock orders and cash, and for handling requests for information;
- JMCO will outsource all Offering agent/data processing/transfer agent functions. The cost of such services will be borne by the Institution and are subject to separate agreement. JMCO will provide the Institution with the proposed agreements for such services prior to the execution of such agreements by JMCO or the Institutions;
- Provide scripts, training and guidance for the telephone team in soliciting proxies and in the stock sales telemarketing effort;
- Educate the Institution's directors, officers and employees about the Reorganization and Offering, their roles and relevant securities laws;
- Train branch managers and customer-contact employees on the proper response to stock purchase inquiries;
- Train and supervise Center staff assisting with proxy and order processing;
- Prepare daily sales reports for management and ensure funds received balance to such reports;
- Coordinate functions with the data processing agent, printer, transfer agent, stock certificate printer and other professionals;
- Design and implement procedures for handling IRA and Keogh orders; and
- Provide post-offering subscriber assistance and management of the pro-ration process.

c. Securities Marketing Services—JMCO uses various sales techniques including direct mail, advertising, community investor meetings, telephone solicitation, and if necessary, selling group formation. The sales approach is tailored to fit your specific situation. Our techniques are designed to attract a stockholder base comprised largely of community oriented individuals loyal to the Institution.

   Our specific actions include:

- Assign licensed registered representatives from our staff to work at the Center to solicit orders on behalf of the Institution from eligible prospects who have been targeted as likely and desirable stockholders;
- Assist management in developing a list of potential investors who are viewed as priority prospects;

- Respond to inquiries concerning the Offering and investment opportunities;
- Organize, coordinate and participate in community informational meetings. These meetings are intended to both relieve customer anxiety and attract potential investors. The meetings generate widespread publicity for the Offering while providing local exposure of the Institution and promoting favorable stockholder relations;
- Supervise and conduct a telemarketing campaign to identify prospects from among the Institution's customer base;
- Continually advise management on market conditions and the community's responsiveness to the Offering; and
- If appropriate assemble a selling group of selected local broker-dealers to assist in selling stock during the offering. In so doing, prepare broker "fact sheets" and arrange "road shows" for the purpose of stimulating local interest in the stock and informing the brokerage community of the particulars of the Offering.

4. COMPENSATION

a. Until such time as the Board of Directors adopts a Plan, the Institution shall pay JMCO a quarterly advisory fee of $50,000 per quarter (pro-rated for partial quarters).
b. An advisory and management fee of $100,000 in connection with the advisory and administrative services set forth in section 3.a. and 3.b. hereof (the "Management Fee"); the Management Fee shall be payable as follows: $50,000 upon adoption of the Plan and $50,000 upon the initial filing of the Registration Statement.
c. A fee of one percent (1.00%) of the dollar amount of the Common Stock sold in the Offering. No fee shall be payable pursuant to this subsection in connection with the sale of stock to (i) officers, Directors, employees or immediate family of such persons ("Insiders"); (ii) a charitable foundation associated with the Institution; and (iii) qualified and non-qualified employee benefit plans of the Company or the Insiders.
d. For stock sold by a group of NASD member firms (which will include JMCO) pursuant to a syndicated community offering solely managed by JMCO (the "Selling Group"), a fee equal to one

percent (1.00%), which fee along with the fee payable directly by the Company to selected dealers shall not exceed six percent (6.00%) in the aggregate. In consultation with JMCO, the Company shall be authorized to determine which NASD member firms participate in the syndicated community offering and the extent of their participation. JMCO will not commence sales of the stock through members of the Selling Group without the specific prior approval of the Company.

Unless otherwise stated all fees described in subparagraphs a, b, c, and d above are to be paid to JMCO at the closing of the Conversion. If, pursuant to a re-solicitation undertaken by the Institution, JMCO is required to provide significant additional services, the parties shall mutually agree to the dollar amount of the additional compensation due (if any).

e. The term of this engagement shall be for a period of one year, unless JMCO's services are terminated earlier by the Company or JMCO at any time with or without cause effective upon receipt of written notice to that effect; provided, however, that JMCO shall perform the related services and will be entitled to the applicable advisory and other fees set forth in subparagraphs b, c, and d above in the event that at any time prior to the expiration of twelve months after such termination an agreement for a Transaction is entered into.

f. If, after adoption of the Plan, (i) the Plan is abandoned or terminated by the Institution; (ii) the Offering is not consummated by March 31, 2004; (iii) JMCO terminates this relationship because there has been a material adverse change in the financial condition or operations of the Institution since September 30, 2002; or (iv) immediately prior to commencement of the Offering, JMCO terminates this relationship because in its opinion, which shall have been formed in good faith after reasonable determination and consideration of all relevant factors, there has been a failure to satisfactorily disclose all relevant information in the disclosure documents or the existence of market conditions which might render the sale of the shares by the Institution hereby contemplated inadvisable; JMCO shall not be entitled to the fees set forth above under subparagraphs c and d, but in addition to quarterly fees already earned pursuant to subparagraph a, the first $50,000 installment under subparagraph b, and reimbursement of its reasonable out-of-pocket expenses as set forth in paragraph 7 below, shall be entitled to receive for its advisory and administrative services the second installment of $50,000 under subparagraph b.

5. MARKET MAKING

If applicable, JMCO agrees to use its best efforts to maintain a market and to solicit other broker-dealers to make a market in the Common Stock after the Offering so that there are at least three market makers for the Common Stock after the Offering.

6. DOCUMENTS

The Institution and its counsel will complete, file with the appropriate regulatory authorities and, as appropriate, amend from time to time, the information to be contained in the Institution's applications to banking and securities regulators and any related exhibits thereto. In this regard, the Institution and its counsel will prepare a prospectus and any other necessary disclosure documents relating to the offering of the Common Stock in conformance with applicable rules and regulations. As the Institution's financial advisor, JMCO will in conjunction with counsel conduct an examination of the relevant documents and records of the Institution and will make such other reasonable investigation as deemed necessary and appropriate under the circumstances. The Institution agrees to make all such documents, records, and other information deemed necessary by JMCO, or its counsel, available to them upon reasonable request. JMCO's counsel will prepare, subject to the approval of the Institution's counsel, the Definitive Agreement. JMCO's counsel shall be selected by RBCO, subject to the approval of the Institution.

7. EXPENSES AND REIMBURSEMENT

The Institution will bear all of its expenses in connection with the Reorganization and the Offering of its Common Stock including, but not limited to, the Institution's attorney fees, NASD filing fees, "blue sky" legal fees, expenses for appraisal, auditing and accounting services, advertising expenses, printing expenses, "road show" expenses, syndicate related expenses, temporary personnel expenses, and the preparation of stock certificates. In the event JMCO incurs such expenses on behalf of the Institution, the Institution shall pay or reimburse JMCO for such reasonable fees and expenses regardless of whether the Reorganization is successfully completed. RBCO will not incur any single expense of more than $2000, pursuant to this paragraph without the prior approval of the Institution.

The Institution also agrees to reimburse JMCO for reasonable out-of-pocket expenses, including legal fees and expenses, incurred by JMCO in connection with the services contemplated hereunder. JMCO will not incur legal fees (excluding the out-of-pocket expenses of counsel) in excess of $100,000 without the approval of the Institution. JMCO will not incur reimbursable direct out of pocket expenses in excess of $35,000 without the consent of the Institution. The parties acknowledge, however, that such cap may be increased by the mutual consent of the Institution and JMCO in the event of any material delay in the Offering, which would require an update of the financial information in tabular form contained in the Prospectus for a period later than that set forth in the original Prospectus filing. Not later than three days before closing, we will provide you with a detailed accounting of all reimbursable expenses to be paid at closing.

8. BLUE SKY

To the extent required by applicable state law, JMCO and the Institution will need to obtain or confirm exemptions, qualifications, or registration of the Common Stock under applicable state securities laws and NASD policies. The cost of such legal work and related filing fees will be paid by the Institution to the law firm furnishing such legal work. The Institution will cause the counsel performing such services to prepare a Blue Sky memorandum related to the Offering including JMCO's participation therein and shall furnish JMCO a copy thereof addressed to JMCO or upon which such counsel shall state JMCO may rely.

9. AVAILABILITY OF "STARS" PROGRAM

As an additional service to the Institution, JMCO will make available for a period of 1 year following the completion of the Offering, advisory services through the JMCO Strategic Advisory Services ("STARS") program. The undersigned will serve as the senior relationship manager for this program. If the Institution elects to avail itself of the STARS program, JMCO will meet with the Institution at its request. JMCO also will provide opinions and recommendations, upon request, for the areas covered below:

- Valuation Analysis
- Merger and Acquisition Planning and Analysis
- Merger and Acquisition Trends
- Planning, Forecasting and Competitive Strategy
- Capital, Asset and Liability Structure and Management

- Stock Repurchase Programs
- Dividend Policy
- Dividend Reinvestment Programs
- Market Development and Sponsorship of Bank Securities
- Financial Disclosure
- Financial Relations
- Financial Reports
- Branch Sales and Purchases
- Stock Benefit Plan Analysis and Advisory
- Stockholder and Investor Relations Presentations and Programs
- Fairness Opinions
- Scanning of Potential Acquisition Candidates
- Based on Published Statement Information

  (This screening does not extend to any in-depth merger and acquisition analyses or studies, which are available under JMCO's normal fee schedule, and does not include retention of JMCO by the Institution for any specific merger/acquisition situation.)

If the Institution elects to utilize the STARS program JMCO will waive the regular retainer fee and hourly charges for this program for the first year. The Institution also will reimburse JMCO's reasonable out-of-pocket expenses incurred in conjunction with the performance of these services. Such out-of-pocket expenses shall include travel, legal, and other miscellaneous expenses. JMCO will not incur any single expense in excess of $2000 pursuant to this paragraph without the prior approval of the Institution.

10. INDEMNIFICATION

The Definitive Agreement will provide for indemnification of the type usually found in underwriting agreements as to certain liabilities, including liabilities under the Securities Act of 1933. The Institution also agrees to defend, indemnify, and hold harmless JMCO and its officers, directors, employees, and agents against all claims, losses, actions, judgments, damages, or expenses, including but not limited to reasonable attorneys' fees, arising solely out of the engagement described herein, except that such indemnification shall not apply to JMCO's own bad faith, willful misconduct, or gross negligence.

11. CONFIDENTIALITY

To the extent consistent with legal requirements and except as otherwise set forth in the Prospectus, all information given to JMCO by the Institution, unless publicly available or otherwise available to JMCO without restriction to breach of any confidentiality agreement ("Confidential Information"), will be held by JMCO in confidence and will not be disclosed to anyone other than JMCO's agents without the Institution's prior approval or used for any purpose other than those referred to in this engagement letter. Upon any termination of its engagement, JMCO shall promptly deliver to the Institution all materials specifically produced for it and will return to the Institution all Confidential Information provided to JMCO during the course of its engagement hereunder.

12. NASD MATTERS

JMCO has an obligation to file certain documents and to make certain representations to the National Association of Security Dealers ("NASD") in connection with the Offering. The Institution agrees to cooperate with JMCO and provide such information as may be necessary for JMCO to comply with all NASD requirements applicable to it in connection with its participation as contemplated herein in the Offering. JMCO is and will remain through completion of the Offering a member in a good standing of the NASD and will comply with all applicable NASD requirements.

13. OBLIGATIONS

(a) Except as set forth below, this engagement letter is merely a statement of intent. While JMCO and the Institution agree in principle to the contents hereof and propose to proceed promptly and in good faith to work out the arrangements with respect to the Offering, any legal obligations between JMCO and the Institution shall be only: (i) those set forth herein in paragraphs 2, 3, and 4 regarding services and payments; (ii) those set forth in paragraph 7 regarding reimbursement for certain expenses; (iii) those set forth in paragraph 10 regarding indemnification; (iv) those set forth in paragraph 11 regarding confidentiality; and (v) as set forth in a duly negotiated and executed Definitive Agreement.

(b) The obligation of JMCO to enter into the Definitive Agreement shall be subject to there being, in JMCO's opinion, which shall have been formed in good faith after reasonable determination and consideration of all relevant factors: (i) no material adverse change in the condition or operation of the Institution; (ii) satisfactory disclosure of all relevant information in the disclosure documents and a determination that the sale of stock is reasonable given such disclosures; (iii) no market conditions which might render the sale of the shares by the Institution hereby contemplated inadvisable; and (iv) agreement that the price established by the independent appraiser is reasonable in the then prevailing market conditions.

14. INDEPENDENT CONTRACTOR; NO FIDUCIARY DUTY

The Company acknowledges and agrees that it is a sophisticated business enterprise and that JMCO has been retained pursuant to this Agreement to act as financial advisor to the Company solely with respect to the matters set forth herein. In such capacity, JMCO shall act as an independent contractor, and any duties of JMCO arising out of this engagement pursuant to this Agreement shall be contractual in nature and shall be owed solely to the Company. Each party disclaims any intention to impose any fiduciary duty on the other.

15. GOVERNING LAW

This Agreement shall be governed by and construed in accordance with the laws of the State of New York applicable to contracts executed and to be wholly performed therein without giving effects to its conflicts of laws principles or rules. Any dispute here under shall be brought in a court in the State of New York.

16. WAIVER of TRAIL BY JURY

EACH OF JMCO AND THE COMPANY WAIVES ALL RIGHT TO TRIAL BY JURY IN ANY ACTION, PROCEEDING, CLAIM, OR COUNTERCLAIM (WHETHER BASED ON CONTRACT, TORT, OR OTHERWISE) RELATED TO OR ARISING OUT OF THIS AGREEMENT.

JONI MUELLER & CO., INC.

BY:______________________________

Patrick Pearl
Chairman & Chief Executive Officer

Accepted and Agreed to This_______ Day of__________, 2020

EAST LONDON SAVINGS BANK

By:____

Penelope Richards
Chairman, President & Chief Executive Officer

Annex E: M&A Contract

(continued)

(continued)

Glossary of Terms

Acquirer *The firm that is purchasing a company in an acquisition—the buyer.*

Acquisition The purchasing company acquires more than 50% of the shares of the acquired company and both companies survive.

Asset Deal The acquirer purchases only the assets of the target company (not its shares).

Asset valuation is the process of determining the fair market **value** of an **asset**. Asset valuation often consists of both subjective and objective measurements.

Beta Beta is a measure of the volatility—or systematic risk—of a security or portfolio compared to the market as a whole. Beta is used in the capital asset pricing model (CAPM), which describes the relationship between systematic risk and expected return for assets (usually stocks).

Bid Price This is the quoted bid, or the highest price at which an investor is willing to buy a security. Available price at which an investor can sell shares of stock.

Book value is the accounting value of the company's assets less all claims senior to common equity (such as the company's liabilities). ... It serves as the total value of the company's assets that shareholders would theoretically receive if a company were liquidated.

Bootstrapping is the process of building a business from scratch without attracting investment or with minimal external capital. It is a way to finance small businesses by purchasing and using resources at the

F. Lessambo, *U.S. Mergers and Acquisitions*,
https://doi.org/10.1007/978-3-030-85735-6

owner's expense, without sharing equity or borrowing huge sums of money from banks.

Business Valuation The act or process of determining the value of a business enterprise or ownership interest therein.

Buyout Purchase of a controlling interest or percent of shares of a company's stock. A leveraged buyout is conducted with borrowed money.

Capital structure is the particular combination of debt and equity used by a company to finance its overall operations and growth. Debt comes in the form of bond issues or loans, while equity may come in the form of common stock, preferred stock, or retained earnings.

CAPM is widely used as a method for pricing risky securities and for generating estimates of the expected returns of assets, considering both the risk of those assets and the cost of capital.

Cash Consideration The portion of the purchase price given to the target in the form of cash.

Cash flow is the net amount of cash and cash-equivalents being transferred into and out of a business. At the most fundamental level, a company's ability to create value for shareholders is determined by its ability to generate positive cash flows, or more specifically, maximize long-term free cash flow.

Conglomerate A merger of companies with seemingly unrelated businesses.

Corporate Governance is a system of rules, policies, and practices that dictate how a company's board of directors manages and oversees the operations of a company.

Corporate Social Responsibility is a type of business self-regulation with the aim of being socially accountable. There is no one "right" way companies can practice CSR; many corporate CSR initiatives strive to positively contribute to the public, the economy or the environment.

Cost of debt is the return that a company provides to its debtholders and creditors. It also reflects the level of interest rates in the market. In addition, it is an integral part of calculating a company's Weighted Average Cost of Capital or WACC.

Covenant A contractual obligation to do or not do something in the future. For example, an affirmative covenant could be to provide quarterly reports to investors, and a negative covenant could prohibit entering into another financing without enabling existing investors to participate.

Deal Structure The nature of the fee paid by the acquiring entity in a merger transaction. Typical deal structure may include stock or other valuables besides cash. The complex nature of deal structure is an important reason why middle market intermediaries are often hired.

Discount rate the interest rate used to determine the present value of future cash flows in a discounted cash flow (DCF) analysis. This helps determine if the future cash flows from a project or investment will be worth more than the capital outlay needed to fund the project or investment in the present.

Discounted Cash Flow is a valuation method used to estimate the value of an investment based on its expected future cash flows. DCF analysis attempts to figure out the value of an investment today, based on projections of how much money it will generate in the future.

Due diligence a comprehensive appraisal of a business undertaken by a prospective buyer, especially to establish its assets and liabilities and evaluate its commercial potential.

Earn out is a contractual provision stating that the seller of a business is to obtain additional compensation in the future if the business achieves certain financial goals, which are usually stated as a percentage of gross sales or earnings.

Economies of Scale Fixed costs decrease because merged companies can eliminate departments with repetitive functions.

Economies of Scope A gain of more specialized skills or technology due to a merger.

Fair Market Value The price, expressed in terms of cash equivalents, at which property would change hands between a hypothetical willing and able buyer, and a hypothetical willing and able seller, acting at arms' length in an open and unrestricted market, when neither is under compulsion to buy or sell and when both have reasonable knowledge of the relevant facts.

Free cash flow is the cash a company produces through its operations, less the cost of expenditures on assets. In other words, free cash flow (FCF) is the cash left over after a company pays for its operating expenses and capital expenditures.

Friendly Takeover The board of directors and management of the target company approve of the takeover. They will advise the shareholders to accept the offer.

Hostile Takeover The board of directors and management of the target company do not approve of the takeover. They will advise the shareholders not to accept the offer.

Identifiable Assets An asset that can be assigned a fair value; can include both tangible and intangible assets.

Intrinsic Value The estimated value of a business using discounted cash flow analysis (often on a per share basis).

Investment Banker A firm that raises capital, trades in securities, or facilities or brokers mergers and acquisitions (or a combination of some or all of these).

Market (Market-Based) Approach A general way of determining a value indication of a business, business ownership interest, security, or intangible asset by using one or more methods that compare the subject to similar businesses, business ownership interests, securities, or intangible assets that have been sold.

Merger is a combination of two or more business entities* in which the assets and liabilities of all the entities are transferred to one, which continues in existence, while all the others cease to exist. Inventory, equipment, stock, and fixtures are tangible items while intangible items may be goodwill, the name or patents.

Merger/Statutory The purchasing company acquires all of the target company shares/assets; the target company ceases to exist (acquirer survives).

Multiple is a comparables analysis method that seeks to value similar companies using the same financial metrics. Enterprise value multiples and equity multiples are the two categories of valuation multiples.

Net asset value is the book value of tangible assets, less intangible assets and liabilities.

Offer Price The price offered per share by the acquirer.

Other Closing Costs This may include due diligence fees, legal fees, accounting fees, etc., related to the deal.

Private equity is an alternative investment class and consists of capital which is not listed on a public exchange. Private equity is composed of funds and investors that directly invest in private companies, or that engage in buyouts of public companies, resulting in the delisting of public equity

Subsidiary Acquirer completely takes over the target but preserves the target's brand for the sake of brand reputation or customer base.

Synergy is the interaction or cooperation of two or more organizations, substances, or other agents to produce a combined effect greater than the sum of their separate effects.

Takeover Premium The percentage above the target's current share price (or VWAP) the offer price represents.

Target The firm that is being acquired (the seller).

Term Sheet A document that outlines the key terms of a proposed transaction. The term sheet is typically non-binding, except for certain provisions.

Terminal value is the value of a business or project beyond the forecast period when future cash flows can be estimated. Terminal value assumes a business will grow at a set growth rate forever after the forecast period.

Valuation is a quantitative process of determining the fair value of an asset or a firm. In general, a company can be valued on its own on an absolute basis, or else on a relative basis compared to other similar companies or assets.

Valuation Approach A general way of determining a value indication of a business, business ownership interest, security, or intangible asset using one or more valuation methods.

Valuation Date The specific point in time when the valuator's opinion of value applies (also referred to as Effective Date or Appraisal Date).

Weighted Average Cost The cost of capital (discount rate) determined by the weighted average, at market value, of the cost of all financing sources in the business enterprise's capital structure.

Working capital is the difference between a company's current assets, such as cash, accounts receivable (customers' unpaid bills) and inventories of raw materials and finished goods, and its current liabilities, such as accounts payable.

Bibliography

Alexandros Prezas, and Karen Simonyan (2015): Corporate divestitures: Spin-offs vs. sell-offs, *Journal of Corporate Finance*, volume 34, pp. 83–107.

Alfred Rappaport and Mark L. Sirower (2016): Stock or Cash?: The Trade-Offs for Buyers and Sellers in Mergers and Acquisitions, *Harvard Business Review*.

Alma Cohen (2013): How do Staggered Boards Affect Shareholder Value? Evidence from a Natural Experiment, *Journal of Financial Economics*, p. 6.

Chris Isidore (2015): GE sells GE Capital unit for $26.5B, CNN Business.

Christina M. Sauter (2020): Delaware as Deal Arbiter, *Washington and Lee Law Review*, volume 77, Issue 3, Article 7, p. 1279.

Christopher M. Bruner (2010): Power and Purpose in the Anglo-American Corporation, *Virginia Journal of International Law*, volume 50, Issue 3, p. 599.

David Harding and Ted Rouse (2007): Human Due Diligence, *Harvard Business Review*.

Elena Vidal (2021): Divestitures, Value Creation, and Corporate Scope, *Strategic Managfement Review*, volume 2, Issue 2, pp. 413–436.

Eva Davis, Kyle Gann, and Rachel Ingwer (2018): Maximizing Value & Minimizing Risks in Carve-Outs: Seller's Pre-Sale Preparation, Winston & Strawn, LLP.

Federal Trade Commission, November 3, 2020.

Franklin R. Edwards (2003): US Corporate Governance: What Went Wrong and Can It Be Fixed?, *Federal Reserve Bank of Chicago Conference*, Nov. 1, 2003, p. 17.

Lucian A. Bebchuk (2002): The Powerful Antitakeover Force of Staggered board, *Stanford Law Review*, 2002, p. 890.

F. Lessambo, *U.S. Mergers and Acquisitions*,
https://doi.org/10.1007/978-3-030-85735-6

Matteo Tonello (2020): Corporate Board Practices in the Russell 3000 and S&P 500, HLS Corporate Governance Forum.

Robert Daines (2016): Can Staggered Boards Improve Value? Evidence from the Massachusetts Natural Experiment, *Stanford Law School.*

Samuel S. Nicholls (2020): The Role of the Investment Banker Compared to the Independent Valuation Analyst in M&A Transactions and Litigation.

Schiller Howard Testimony before the US Senate Committee, p. 10.

Stephen A. Radin (2009): The Business Judgment Rule 3612 (6th ed. 2009) (quoting Midland Food Servs., LLC v. Castle Hill Hldgs. V, LLC, 792 A.2d 920, 931 (Del. Ch.1999) (Strine, V.C.)).

Thomas Bates, Jordan B. Neyland, and Yolanda Yulong Wang (2017): Financing Acquisitions with Earnouts.

US Senate Investigations Committee (July 30, 2015): Impact of the U.S. Tax Code on the Market for Corporate Control and Jobs, Majority Staff report, p. 4.

Wachtell, Lipton, Rosen, & Katz (2013): Spin-Off Guide, pp. 4–5.

Yakov Amihud, Markus Schmid, and Steven D. Solomon (2018): Settling the Staggered Board, *University of Pennsylvania law Review*, volume 166: 1475, p. 1480.

Zohar Goshen and Sharon Hannes (2028): The Death of Corporate law, ECGI, Law Working Paper No. 402/2018, p. 14.

Index

F. Lessambo, *U.S. Mergers and Acquisitions*,
https://doi.org/10.1007/978-3-030-85735-6

The manufacturer's authorised representative in the EU is Springer Nature Customer Service Centre GmbH, Europaplatz 3, 69115 Heidelberg, Germany. If you have any concerns regarding our products, please contact ProductSafety@springernature.com

Printed and bound by CPI Group (UK) Ltd, Croydon, CR0 4YY
30/09/2026
02225704-0003